THE HISTORY
OF THE JEWS

BY

Gotthard Deutsch, Ph.D.

PROFESSOR OF HISTORY, HEBREW UNION
COLLEGE

NEW YORK
BLOCH PUBLISHING COMPANY
1910

TABLE OF CONTENTS

PREFACE

THERE are two main difficulties confronting the historian, when he attempts to write history. He must always ask himself, First: Are the facts which I find recorded really facts, and Second: Do I interpret them correctly? Thiers, in his "Histoire du Consulat," Paris, 1851, Vol. XI, p. 71, speaks of the enthusiasm with which the Jews of Portugal, who numbered 200,000, received the French troops in 1809. There were perhaps not two hundred Jews living in Portugal at that time, and they played no part in public affairs. In an address to the convention of the Order Brith Abraham, Mayor Gaynor, of New York, said on May 15, 1910: "The great Frederick issued a general privilege, and declared it as a maxim, that oppression of the Jews never brought prosperity to any state, and Napoleon not only followed the same course but convoked the Sanhedrin." The facts are in the main correct, but the presentation is all wrong. Frederick issued his "Revidierte Generalprivilegium" of April 17, 1750, for the Jews of Prussia, but it is based on the mediæval idea of restrictions in the most elementary rights of human beings. His sentiment with regard to the Jews is evident from a letter which he wrote to the Minister von Hoym, May 17, 1780, in which he says: "If the Jews were expelled and Christians would take their places as innkeepers, it would be for the good of the country, and we would have more human beings and less Jews" (*Monatsschrift fuer die Geschichte und Wissenschaft des Judentums,* 1895, p. 379). Napoleon had by the convocation of the "Assembly of Jewish Notables" and the subse-

5

quent Sanhedrin, 1806-1807, insulted the Jews. The law of September 27, 1791, had declared them as citizens, and he asked them whether they considered France as their fatherland, and when these and similar questions were answered in the affirmative with emphatic protestation of loyalty, Napoleon nevertheless reintroduced the mediæval principle of Jewish disabilities by issuing laws restricting Jews in doing business on credit. The facts quoted by Mayor Gaynor prove the opposite of what he wished to prove by them.

These instances taken from Jewish history could be multiplied endlessly from every period and every section of the world's history. Jewish history has to contend with two additional difficulties. It extends over every part of the civilized world, but it lacks chronological sequence, at least until we come to modern times. Another difficulty is that it deals with almost every known spiritual activity of mankind. The student, in order to understand Jewish history, should know the constantly shifting boundary lines of the Italian states from mediæval times until 1870, and he should know something of the morphological theories of Hebrew grammer and of scholastic philosophy.

These difficulties make themselves especially felt in a brief manual, and, no doubt, every teacher of Jewish history must have had such an experience. The Rabbis (Sanhedrin 93, b) find fault with Nehemiah for having spoken ill of his predecessors in office (Neh. V, 15). I do not wish to incur the same censure. It remains for the student and the teacher who use my book to judge whether I improved upon my predecessors. My object was to place in the hand of the student, who is guided by a capable teacher, a concise and yet readable manual of the whole post-biblical history. The biblical period I intentionally omitted, in order to avoid contested ground and to allow the book to be used in all schools regardless of dogmatic differences.

GOTTHARD DEUTSCH.

CINCINNATI, O., July, 1910.

HISTORY OF THE JEWS

CHAPTER I

FROM THE BABYLONIAN CAPTIVITY (586 B.C.) TO THE DESTRUCTION OF THE SECOND TEMPLE (70 C.E.)

PALESTINE, the buffer state between Egypt and Mesopotamia, the two rival powers of the ancient world, was an important base of operations for all conquerors, and its possession was eagerly sought. In 722 B.C., King Sargon of Assyria conquered the northern part, the kingdom of Israel. The southern part, the kingdom of Judah, was at that time protected by Assyria's rising and already powerful rival, the Babylonian empire. When Babylonia had become the master of Mesopotamia, Judæa's doom was sealed, and in 586 Nebuchadnezzar captured Jerusalem and made all of Palestine a province of his large empire.

With the death of Nebuchadnezzar, the great Babylonian empire declined rapidly, and in 539, Cyrus, the King of Persia, captured the city of Babylon, and became the master of the whole of the Babylonian empire, and so of Palestine. He was favorably inclined to the Jews, and gave permission to the descendants of the exiles from Palestine to return to the land of their fathers. Only a few thousand made use of this, and returned under the leadership of Zerubbabel, a descendant of the House of David, and of Joshua ben Jehozadak, the high priest.   Of the right to build the Temple they made no use for the time, but erected instead an altar on the site of the former edifice.   The development of the new commonwealth, however, was slow, until Ezra, a man learned in the law, and, therefore, called the Scribe, returned from Babylonia in 458 B.C. and taught the people the law of God.   He was joined in 445 B.C. by Nehemiah, the cupbearer of the Persian King Artaxerxes, who received permission from his ruler to go to Palestine and assist Ezra in his work.   He succeeded, after many difficulties, in rebuilding the walls of Jerusalem and giving the new community a firm organization.   In 432 B.C. he returned to his post at the King's Court, but upon learning that the new community was suffering from many difficulties, he returned again to Palestine to finish his work there.

It seems that the Jews lived in peace, for during the following century, while they were under Persian rule, only two incidents are recorded.   In the reign of Artaxerxes III, Ochus (358–337 B.C.), the Jews rebelled; but the king defeated them near Jericho and sent the rebels to Hyrcania into exile.   About the same time the high priest, Johanan, killed his brother, Joshua, in the Temple, and the Persian governor fined the Jews very heavily.

Not long afterwards the mighty Persian empire was conquered by Alexander the Great (333 B.C.), and the Jews passed under the rule of the Macedonian king.

There are various legends about Alexander's kindness to the Jews, especially one which states that he showed great respect to the high priest. There is also a report that he exempted the Jews from paying taxes in the Sabbatical year. His immense empire fell to pieces soon after his early death, and various generals fought for a portion of the inheritance, each expecting to become the successor of the great conqueror. Palestine with Syria was first occupied by Ptolemy, who founded the dynasty named after him in Egypt in 320 B.C. He lost it to another general, Antigonus (315 B.C.), who was defeated by Seleucus at the battle of Gaza (312 B.C.), after which the kingdom of Syria with Antioch as its capital was founded. The Syrians counted their era from this date and the Jews adopted this custom, keeping it up until late in mediæval times. The struggle continued until, in 301 B.C, the battle of Ipsus decided the issue in favor of Ptolemy and Palestine was united with Egypt until Antiochus III of Syria annexed it to his dominions in 198 B.C.

The Jews seem to have been treated with fairness until Antiochus IV, Epiphanes (175-164 B.C.), succeeded his father. The latter had been defeated by the Romans in the battle of Magnesia (189 B.C.), and Antiochus IV was sent as hostage to Rome. Knowing that the Romans watched the growth of the Syrian kingdom with great jealousy lest it should become a powerful rival, he tried to consolidate his states and for this reason wished to remove everything which kept the Jews apart from their neighbors. In his attempt to Hellenize the Jews he was supported by a party among them. Joseph, the son of Tobias, and the nephew of Onias II, the High Priest, had already under the Egyptian kings been appointed tax collector

and was very powerful. He and his family supported the Syrian kings in their desire to Hellenize the
Jews.

Simon, a member of this family, quarrelled with the
High Priest, Onias III, and in order to revenge himself he informed the Syrian government that the Temple of Jerusalem contained large treasures. Heliodorus
was sent to Jerusalem, but for some reason which
legend has obscured by miraculous tales, he was prevented from looting the treasury. Onias was called
to Antioch to answer certain charges of disloyalty,
while his brother Joshua, or Jason as he called himself, took his place. Jason offered Antiochus a higher
tribute than his brother had paid, and declared his
willingness to support the king in introducing Greek
customs among the Jews. He became high priest,
but shortly afterwards Menelaus, another member of
the family, offered Antiochus a still higher tribute and
was made high priest in Jason's place. Unable to pay
the sum he had promised, he appropriated valuable
pieces from the Temple treasury to bribe the King's
officials. Onias reproached him and was assassinated
upon his order.

This fact embittered the Jews. Menelaus was
charged with sacrilege, but as he possessed great influence the case was dismissed and his opponents were
executed. These events enraged the Jews still more,
and when in 170 B.C., Antiochus was in Egypt engaged in warfare, the Jews rebelled at the false report
of his death. Antiochus returned and took bitter
revenge, pillaging the city, and desecrating the Temple. Two years later he sent his general, Apollo-
nius, to punish the rebels and the latter did it in the

most cruel manner. At the same time a strong fort was built in Jerusalem and the practice of the Jewish religion, particularly the observance of the Sabbath and the dietary laws, and the study of the Torah prohibited, on the ground that they tended to keep the Jews aloof from their neighbors. At the same time an altar to Zeus was erected in the Temple and other heathenish altars placed in various cities. The Jews were compelled under penalty of death to offer sacrifices to the Greek gods.

The pious people fled from Jerusalem into the wilderness in order to escape the fulfillment of the king's orders. Among the leaders of those who were determined rather to die than give up their religion was Mattathiah, an aged priest of the family of the Hasmonæans. In the little town of Modin he killed a Jew who made preparations to offer sacrifice on the heathenish altar, and an officer was sent to execute the king's decree. This was the signal for rebellion. Mattathiah had five sons of whom Judah, called the Maccabee, was the leader in battle. Judah gathered a small number of the faithful around him and succeeded in defeating various generals and finally the viceroy, Lysias. Then he entered Jerusalem, removed all traces of idolatry from the Temple and rededicated it to the service of God in 165 B.C. Shortly afterwards, in 164 B.C., Antiochus IV died and was succeeded by his son, Antiochus V, still a boy, for whom Lysias governed as regent. The last having many difficulties to contend with, granted the Jews religious freedom. He and the young king, however, were soon killed, and Demetrius I, a nephew of Antiochus IV, came to the throne in 162 B.C.

Demetrius continued to give the Jews religious freedom, but he appointed a high priest named Alkymus,
whom the people disliked, and so the rebellion started
anew. Judah defeated the general Nikanor in 161
B.C., but a year later he fell in battle and was succeeded by his brother Jonathan. Meantime Syria was
torn to pieces amid constant rebellion caused by
various claimants to the throne, each of whom tried
to win the Jews over to his side in order to obtain a
free hand in fighting his rivals. Thus Jonathan was
confirmed as high priest by the Syrian king (153 B.C.),
but later on, being distrusted, was assassinated by the
Syrian governor, Tryphon (143 B.C.) He was succeeded by the last surviving son of Mattathiah, Simon
(143–135 B.C.). Simon drove the Syrian garrison from
the fort at Jerusalem and was not only confirmed as
high priest but also as ruler of the Jews. He manifested his sovereignty by issuing coins bearing his
name.

The Romans, who were glad to see the power of the
Syrian king weakened, formed an alliance with him,
and so Israel was again an independent nation.
Simon was assassinated by Ptolemy, his own son-in-
law, and was succeeded by his son John Hyrcan
(135–105 B.C.), who assumed the title of king and
was at the same time the high priest. The Syrian
kingdom became altogether dismembered, and John
Hyrcan, aided by the Romans, united under his scep-
tre not only the Jews living in Palestine but also conquered those parts of the country which were inhabited
by other nations. The Idumæans and the Samaritans
were forcibly converted to Judaism. With the growing power of the new kingdom the religious life of the

ruling classes became weakened and the king alienated those people who had formerly been the most zealous supporters of the Maccabæan rebellion. Two parties were formed, one called the Sadducees, after the High Priest Zadok, was in sympathy with the government while the other, the Pharisees, became its opponent. The Pharisees (separatists) believed in freedom only as a means of protection of their religious life, and therefore opposed the king, who wasted the resources of the country in wars of conquest.

Hyrcan was succeeded by Aristobul, his son, with whose reign a period of family feuds and palace intrigues began. He ordered his brother Antigonus to be killed and died soon afterwards, having reigned but one year (105–104 B.C.). His successor was his brother Alexander Jannai (104–78 B.C.). The latter's highest ambition was to become a conqueror and he carried on constant but unsuccessful warfare with Arabic chieftains, and with the Egyptians and other neighbors. The people rebelled against him, but he quelled all uprisings with extreme cruelty, and on one occasion had six hundred pilgrims massacred in the courtyard of the Temple. The Pharisees were particularly the objects of his hatred.

Upon his death his wife, Salome Alexandra, came to the throne (78-69 B.C.). She made peace with the Pharisees, whose leader Simeon ben Shetach was her brother, and her reign was happier than that of her husband. Upon her death she left two sons, Hyrcan II and Aristobul, of whom the first was to be high priest, while the second was to be king. But they soon quarrelled, and Hyrcan, who was a tool in the hands of Antipater, an Idumæan, his adviser, declared

himself king. In the subsequent civil war, Pompey,
the Roman general and statesman, was asked to act as
arbitrator. He conquered Jerusalem, entered the
Temple, and declared in favor of Hyrcan, who, however, was not made king, but given the title of
Ethnarch. Aristobul was sent to Rome and the cities
inhabited by Syrians were annexed to the province of
Syria (60 B.C.). Aristobul's son, Alexander, the son-
in-law of Hyrcan, rebelled, but was defeated in 57 B.C.
In the following year Aristobul fled from Rome and
organized a rebellion, but was soon defeated and sent
a prisoner to Rome with his son Antigonus.

Crassus, governor of Syria, entered the Temple and
looted the treasury (54 B.C.). Shortly afterwards he
fell in battle and the Jews rebelled again, but the
uprising was cruelly suppressed, 30,000 being sold
into slavery (53 B.C.). Cæsar, who was now the ruler
of Rome, liberated Aristobul to use him against his
rival Pompey, but Aristobul was poisoned and his son
Alexander executed (49 B.C.). Hyrcan and Antipater
joined Cæsar, who confirmed the former as Ethnarch
and bestowed high distinction on the latter (47 B.C.).
Antipater's son, Herod, was made governor of Galilee,
and as such executed the insurgent leader, Hezekiah,
and put down the rebellion. Called before the Sanhedrin for executing a citizen without trial, he defied
the court, knowing that he had the support of the
Romans. After Cæsar's assassination Antipater joined
Cassius, but was himself assassinated (42 B.C.). His
sons, however, remained in power, and after the battle of Philippi they joined Antony, who confirmed
them as governors (42 B.C.). Antigonus, the son of
Aristobul, now returned, assisted by the Parthians,

enemies of Rome, and was made high priest, combining again the dignity of king and high priest (40–37 B.C.). Herod fled to Rome, where he was appointed King of the Jews by the Senate. Returning to Palestine he defeated Antigonus and reigned as king (37–34 B.C.). He married Mariamne, the granddaughter of Hyrcan and Aristobul, and appointed her brother, Aristobul, as high priest. Becoming jealous of his popularity, he caused him to be assassinated soon afterward.

Herod's reign was marked by its splendor, but he was hated by the people for his extreme cruelty. He had his wife, Mariamne, three of his sons, the old High Priest Hyrcan II, and various other members of his family, assassinated. His unpopularity grew in spite of the fact that the country was prosperous and that he rebuilt the Temple in magnificent style. As a descendant of the Idumæans, whom Hyrcan I had converted to Judaism, he was considered a foreigner who held his power only through the assistance of Rome. From this time the name Edom became a synonym for Rome in Jewish Literature.

Herod left three sons, Archelaus, Herod Antipas, and Philip, among whom he divided his empire. Archelaus received Judæa, Samaria and Idumæa. He was to reside in Jerusalem and have the title of king. Herod Antipas was given dominion over Galilee, and Peræa and Philip received the northern district; both were to be called Tetrarchs. In Archelaus' kingdom a revolt broke out at once, and 3,000 people were killed in the Temple courtyard. When he went to Rome to obtain confirmation of his title another rebellion broke out because of the cruelty of the Roman commander, and once more a great number of people were killed and the Temple sacked. Governor Varus was called from Syria to quell the contest and did so with great cruelty. The Roman Emperor Augustus confirmed Archelaus as ruler of Judæa but refused him the title of king; he was merely called Ethnarch. Unable to control the people, who hated him, he was deposed and exiled to Gaul, and his land made a part of the Roman province of Syria (6 C.E.). The Roman governors carried on an arbitrary and oppressive rule. A census ordered by Quirinius was bitterly resisted and almost led to open rebellion. A party of Zealots was formed under the leadership of Judah, the son of Hezekiah, whom Herod had executed. Their object was to overthrow the Roman rule, and for this purpose they began a reign of terror against all people who were supposed to be in sympathy with Rome, and assassinations were of daily occurrence.

One of the most cruel of the Roman governors, Pontius Pilate (26–36), in every possible way provoked the religious sentiments of the people, and on the slightest show of resistance, ordered wholesale butcheries of them. Many complaints were sent to Rome and he was finally recalled. Under his administration the execution of Jesus is reported to have taken place. Emperor Caligula (37–41), a typical megalomaniac, ordered his bust placed in the Temple. Petronius, the military commander, reported that it was impossible to execute this order without driving the people into open rebellion, and so Caligula modified his demand. Only his assassination prevented an outbreak of the people. He was a friend of Agrippa, the son of Aristobul, and the grandson of Herod and Mariamne, and showered his favors

upon him.   Agrippa was first appointed the successor
of his uncle Philip with the title of king, in 37.   Upon
the death of Herod Antipas, Galilee was added to his
dominion, and finally Emperor Claudius, upon his
succession to the throne in 41, gave him Judæa also,
so that he thus obtained the full heritage of his grandfather Herod.   While a favorite of Rome, Agrippa was
beloved by the people, but he died in the prime of his
life in 44.   His brother Herod, who was his successor, possessed no other right except to appoint the
high priest; similarly Agrippa's son, Agrippa II,
while honored with the title of king, had practically
no power.   For at the death of Agrippa I Palestine
was again placed under Roman governors, seven of
whom held office from 44 to 66 and did their utmost
to drive the people into despair by cruel executions
and wanton disregard of religious feeling.   The reign
of terror continuing, a party called Sicarii, from Sica,
a dagger, which they always carried under their garments for the punishment of those who were suspected
of Roman sympathies, arose and spread anarchy all
through the land.

The last of the governors, Gessius Florus, was the
worst of all who held this office.   His extortions and
murders drove the people into despair.   Especially in
Cæsarea, where the majority of the population was
Greek, and constantly attacked the Jews, he refused to
grant them protection.   Agrippa II made an attempt
to pacify the Jews and persuade them to send a committee to Rome, but without avail.   The daily sacrifice on behalf of the Emperor was discontinued and
open rebellion was declared (66).

The Jews fortified the Temple, captured several

Roman forts, including that of Jerusalem, and Cestius Gallus, the commander of Syria, was defeated. Vespasian, the ablest general of the Roman army, was placed in command and began the war in Galilee, where Flavius Josephus, the famous historian, was in command of the revolutionary forces (67). Josephus was besieged in the fortress of Jotapat, and, after weeks of hard fighting, surrendered. In the fall of 67 all of Galilee was in the hands of the Romans.

In 68 Vespasian conquered the land east of the Jordan, while in Jerusalem the reign of terror continued and the Zealots wasted their forces in a bloody civil war. Meantime a revolution had broken out in Rome and Nero had committed suicide (68). Three emperors followed each other in quick succession and the internal troubles caused Vespasian to temporize in his warfare. But by 69 he had conquered the whole land with the exception of Jerusalem and three fortified cities held by the patriots. In this year he was proclaimed Emperor and went to Rome, leaving the work of continuing the war to his son Titus.

Titus began the siege of Jerusalem in April, 70, and at once the internal feuds ceased, the besieged doing their utmost to defend the place. Titus had to take the city step by step. Finally on August 10th the Temple, the last retreat of the patriots, was stormed and destroyed by fire. Those who survived intrenched themselves in the upper city and continued their resistance until September 7th. According to Josephus, 1,100,000 perished in the war and 97,000 were made captives and sold as slaves or taken to the circus, where they were torn to pieces by wild beasts. Seven hundred, selected from the noblest families, were taken to Rome to be shown with the holy vessels captured in the Temple in the triumphal march. An arch of triumph was erected as a memorial of victory, which is still standing in Rome. Titus left the siege of the three remaining fortresses to his captains. They spent three more years in reducing them, Massada, the last one, falling in 73. The last defenders of the place killed themselves in order to escape being taken alive by the Romans. Thus the last vestige of the independent Jewish kingdom, founded by the Maccabees, disappeared.

CHAPTER II

THE destruction of Jerusalem had thrown the Jewish people into a terrible crisis. Although the Jews,
as individuals, did not fare worse than during the preceding one hundred and thirty years, Judæa was now
a province of the Roman Empire.

The only new law, enforced after the destruction of
Jerusalem, was that of a special tax of two Drachmæ,
which every male had to pay. This tax, called
"Fiscus Judaicus," took the place of the half-shekel
formerly paid by every male Jew into the treasury of
the Temple, according to the Rabbinic interpretation
of the Law in Exodus xxx, 11-16. Some of the Jews
were sold into slavery; some went to Rome, where
they swelled the congregation existing there since the
second century B.C., and where they had several
synagogues and catacombs used as cemeteries. Others
again emigrated to Babylonia, where a Jewish settlement existed since the destruction of Jerusalem by
Nebuchadnezzar, or settled on the northern coast of
Africa, and on the islands of the Mediterranean.

Under Domitian, the brother and successor of Titus
(81-96), the tribute of the "Fiscus Judaicus" was
exacted with great severity. Domitian was altogether
hostile to the Jews; yet in his reign Jewish propa-

ganda increased in Rome, and people belonging to the highest class of society, among them Flavius Clemens, a nephew of the Emperor, with his wife Clementina, were converted to Judaism. Flavius Clemens was put to death and his wife exiled for their change of faith, as the Roman law considered it a crime, and called it atheism. Dio Cassius, the historian of Rome, speaks of a class of people who were not Jews by descent, but had adopted the Jewish religion. Similar proofs of the existence of a Jewish propaganda are found in the New Testament (Matthew xxiii, 25) where the Pharisees are denounced for their efforts in making converts, and in the daily service, composed about one hundred, in which a special prayer for the proselytes is offered.

Under Emperor Nerva (96–98) the "Fiscus Judaicus" is said to have been abolished.

Under Trajan (98-117) serious rebellions of the Jews occurred in Egypt, Cyprus, Cyrene, and Mesopotamia. About the causes of the disorder and the battles of the rebellion, we know nothing definite. It may be said, however, that in all likelihood oppressive taxation, cruel treatment of the people by the Roman officials, and the traditional enmity between the Jews and the Greek-speaking population of the Orient were the causes of this constant friction. Trajan sent his general, Quietus, to quell the uprising, and made him governor of Palestine. The insurrection was still in progress when Hadrian came to the throne (117–136). At first he was friendly toward the Jews and began to rebuild the Temple, by which he hoped to reconcile them. This new Temple, however, was to be dedicated to the Jupiter of the Capitol, who, as Hadrian

believed, was also the God of the Jews, although he
had a different name.   As the Jews, however, were
not willing to accept this condition, Hadrian resorted
to severe religious persecution.   He prohibited the
practices of the Sabbath, circumcision, and the study
of the Law.   The result was another rebellion under
the leadership of Simeon Bar Koziba, who adopted the
name of Bar Kochba—"The Son of the Star "—with
reference to the prophecy of the star which would
smite the enemies of Israel (Num. xxiv, 17).   Bar
Kochba, who called himself Prince of Israel, and had
coins struck with his name, was supported by a priest,
Eleazar of Modin, and by Rabbi Akiba.   Details of
this war are unknown.   It lasted, however, over three
years (132–135), and then was quelled by Tineius
Rufus, and Julius Severus, the latter having been called
from Great Britain to take some of the troops against
the rebels.   The victory was complete.   Whatever
had been left of Jerusalem after its destruction by
Titus was destroyed.   The city was called Ælia Capi-
tolina, in honer of Hadrian, whose first name was
Ælius and in honor of the Jupiter of the Capitol, to
whom the Temple, built on the site of the ancient
Temple of Solomon, was erected.   Over one of the
gates of the city Hadrian had the head of a swine
placed, and the Jews were forbidden entrance into the
city.   A great many Jews were killed in battle and
many prisoners, including the most prominent spiritual leaders of the rebellion, such as Rabbi Akiba, executed.   A mediæval legend speaks of ten martyrs,
and gives a list which, however, comprises men who
lived in different ages.

With the death of Hadrian, and the succession to

the throne of Marcus Antoninus Pius (136–161) a change for the better took place. We are informed that, upon the representations of prominent Jews, Antoninus repealed the cruel laws passed by his predecessor. Jewish legends have preserved the name of Antoninus Pius as one of the most benign of rulers, and they represent him as a close personal friend of Judah the Patriarch, as a great admirer of Judaism, and even as a secret convert.

Only a few disconnected facts are known about the following emperors. Under Marcus Aurelius, the philosophic author (161–180), who, in one instance speaks with contempt of the Jews, we hear of a slave, named Callistus, sentenced to penal servitude in the mines of Sardinia for having disturbed the services of a synagogue.

Under Septimius Severus (193–211), we learn of the participation of the Jews in a rebellion, and an edict, passed in 204, declared conversion to Christianity from Judaism a crime. It was evidently intended to check the rapid progress of Christianity. Alexander Severus (222–235) is said to have been very favorable to the Jews, and his mother, [Mammæa, who was regent during the first years of his reign, is said to have been favorably inclined toward the Jewish religion. Alexander had a statue of Abraham in his room and on the wall was inscribed the famous saying of Hillel, "What is hateful unto thee, do not unto thy neighbor." The Jews of Rome had a synagogue which was named the Synagogue of Severus in his honor; he presented to it a scroll of the Torah which had been brought from Jerusalem. The mobs in Alexandria and Antioch, ever hostile to the Jews,

called him Archysynagogos, "leader of the Synagogue."

The spiritual life of the Jews, after the destruction
of the Temple, received its strongest impetus from
Johanan ben Zakkai, in Jabneh (Jamnia), whom legend
makes a disciple of Hillel and a member of the Sanhedrin in Jerusalem at the time of the destruction of
the Temple. Legend further says that he succeeded
in escaping from Jerusalem during the siege at a time
when the Zealots in the city would not allow any one
to leave it, and that he came to Vespasian, to whom
he prophesied his elevation to the throne of Rome, for
which, out of gratitude, the latter allowed him to
open a school and establish a Sanhedrin in Jabneh.
At any rate, Jabneh became the spiritual centre of
Judaism at that time. Various ordinances, which
Johanan ben Zakkai issued, show his desire to harmonize ancient traditions with the conditions as they
developed after the destruction of the Temple. Thus,
it is understood that he ordered the Shofar to be blown
in Jabneh, even if New Year fell on a Sabbath; this
formerly had been done only in the Temple at Jerusalem.

His successor was Gamaliel, usually called Gamaliel II, Gamaliel the elder, or Gamaliel of Jabneh
(100–130). He was the great-great-grandson of the
famous Hillel, who, according to tradition, was president of the Sanhedrin during the time of King Herod
(Hillel, Simeon, Gamaliel, Simeon, Gamaliel). In the
work of harmonizing tradition with the exigencies of
the time, Gamaliel followed in the footsteps of Johanan
ben Zakkai. His main activities consisted in the
organization of public worship. To him is ascribed

the introduction of the daily prayer (Tefillah), the eighteen benedictions (Shemoneh Esreh), to which later in his life he added one more, containing a petition against sectaries (Minim). He also composed the grace after meals, and the Passover Haggadah. He further endeavored, in all possible ways, to strengthen the authority of the President or Nasi or Ab Beth Din of the Sanhedrin, especially by claiming for himself the exclusive right to fix the calendar. In the interpretation of the law he took a lenient attitude, insisting more on the spirit than on the letter.

Opponents of his hierarchical tendencies were Eliezer ben Hyrkanos and Joshua ben Hananiah; Akiba occupied an undecided position between the two parties. Eliezer, who seems to have been favorably inclined toward Christianity, objected to a fixed ritual, but otherwise was rigorous in his interpretation of the law, and a firm believer in the authority of tradition. From obscure reports we learn that he was excommunicated by Gamaliel, his brother-in-law. Joshua was strongly opposed to Christianity, and to the hierarchical tendencies of Gamaliel, and his harsh treatment by the latter caused opposition, with the result that Gamaliel was removed from office and Eleazer ben Azariah appointed in his place. But later on a reconciliation took place, and Gamaliel was reinstated.

Akiba, the disciple of Eliezer, was the strictest opponent of Christianity, and especially of the principle which declares that the law is merely a symbol, and also of the demand that the Jews give up their national distinctiveness. His opposition to the symbolic interpretation of the law led him into its literal interpretation, based on the view that every word and letter of the Torah must be explained independently of the context. He was also a zealous advocate of Israel's national independence, and so became the spiritual leader of the Bar Kochba rebellion. When he said, "Thou shalt love thy neighbor as thyself; this is the fundamental principle of the Torah," he probably gave expression to his nationalistic sentiments. Evidently in order to accentuate the universality of Judaism, Simeon ben Azai, Akiba's contemporary, says that the words, "This is the book of the generation of Adam," are the fundamental principles of the Torah. Rabbi Akiba's principle of interpreting the Torah was opposed by his contemporary, Rabbi Ishmael, who says the Torah speaks the language of men; that is, every text must be explained by its context. An important figure of that time seems to have been Elisha ben Abuyah, who is called Acher the Apostate. The stories told of him are legendary to such an extent that it is impossible to know how much, if any, historical fact underlies them.

The uprising of Bar Kochba and the subsequent prohibition of the study of law interrupted, for a while, the development of religious doctrine. Soon, however, after the succession to the throne of Antoninus Pius, in 136, the study of the law was resumed. A synod of prominent rabbis, who were mostly disciples of Akiba, met at Usha, and passed several resolutions, mostly in regard to civil law, required by the exigencies of the time. One of these provides that every one shall give one-fifth of his income to charity, thus diverting the two tithes formerly devoted to the sacrificial needs, the Levites or the poor, to communal requirements. Another resolution declared that every father was under the duty of providing for his son until the latter was twelve years old. The spiritual leaders of this age were Rabbi Meir, Judah bar Ilai, and Jose bar Halafta, and the office of Nasi was given to Gamaliel's son, Simeon ben Gamaliel II (140–170). The latter was in turn succeeded by his son, Judah Hanasi, called Rabbi, or Rabbenu-Hakadosh, who according to a legend was born on the day on which Rabbi Akiba died (135–216). To him is due the compilation of the Mishnah or compendium of the Rabbinic law.

The word Mishnah is derived from Mishneh Torah (repetition of the law), the name of Deuteronomy. This compilation was preceded by others on a smaller scale which we do not possess. They are called, after their authors, the Mishnah of Rabbi Akiba, that of Rabbi Meir, and that of Rabbi Nathan. The object of the code compiled by Judah Hanasi was to collect the whole of the Rabbinic law. The authorities quoted in the Mishnah are called Tanaim, from תנא, which is the Aramaic, for שנה, the latter being a word derived from Mishnah. The Mishnah was not intended to be a code of the law but a compendium for its study. It was soon, however, accepted as an infallible book of laws, and believed to be based on early tradition dating back to Moses himself.

CHAPTER III

ERA OF THE TALMUD (200–600)

The constant progress made by Christianity in Palestine had an unfavorable effect on the condition of the Jewish population and the Jews began to emigrate to Babylonia in constantly growing numbers. The latter country had, in the meantime, passed from the rule of the Parthians to that of the neo-Persians, or Parsees (225). These having thrown off the yoke of foreign invaders, acted like others under similar conditions and introduced a government marked by religious and national fanaticism, from which the Jews suffered very severely. The Parsees, who worshipped fire, would not allow the Jews to have any light on the Sabbath during their period of mourning, which comprised the shortest winter days, and consequently the Hanukah lights were also forbidden. Another prohibition, which the Jews especially resented, was directed against the burial of the dead, not allowed by the religion of the Parsees.

At the same time, the Roman Empire, passing more and more under Christian rule; became hostile toward the Jews. Of Diocletian (284-305) it is reported that, while he tried to suppress Christianity, he allowed the Jews freedom of worship. Another story reported of him, to the effect that he ordered Judah Hanasi to appear before him on the Sabbath, wishing to punish

28

him for the insult he had suffered from Jewish boys, while a swineherd, is evidently legendary. Constantine (305–337), who removed all the disabilities from which the Christians had suffered, and according to some authors, a professing Christian himself, issued the first edict which discriminated against the Jews. This law prohibited the circumcision of a slave, and there is no doubt that it was intended to check propaganda for Judaism.

Julian the Apostate (361–363), who wished to suppress Christianity and attempted to reintroduce a refined worship of the old gods, is said to have attempted to rebuild the Temple at Jerusalem. The church historians tell us that an earthquake and similar accidents made this impossible. It is, however, not unlikely that the whole report was merely an invention to show that the Temple could never be rebuilt, and that all attempts to fight Christianity must be vain.

The discrimination against the Jews became stronger when Theodosius issued the edict of Ravenna (380), which made the profession of Christianity a requirement for all who held office under the government. After the death of Theodosius the Roman Empire was divided into an Eastern and a Western Empire. Palestine and the majority of the Jews were in the Eastern Empire, with its capital at Constantinople; and they remained subject to this rule until the Holy Land was conquered by the Mohammedans in 634.

The legal treatment of the Jews, in both divisions of the Empire, was hostile, but the authorities tried to protect their lives and properties against the constantly increasing attacks of the mob. Such outbreaks

occurred especially in the Greek cities of the Orient.
Cyril, Bishop of Alexandria, and St. Simeon, the
Stylite, who for years lived on a pillar, stirred up the
religious fanaticism of the masses by setting them
against the Jews. These attacks resulted in loss of
life and property, and when the emperors issued
orders demanding the punishment of the lawless elements, the ecclesiastic leaders condemned this action
as the evidence of partiality toward the Jews. Under
Emperor Justinian (527–565) we hear for the first
time of an interference with the internal religious life
of the Jews by the secular authorities. An edict of
this Emperor prohibited the reading of the Deuterosis
in the synagogue. The word is a literal translation
of the word Mishnah, but as the Mishnah could not
have been read in the synagogue, we must assume
that other Rabbinic works or the Targum are meant.

The Byzantine Empire frequently had wars with its
Persian neighbor, and one of these which threatened
to be very critical occurred under Emperor Heraclius
(622–628). In this, the Jews at first sided with the
Persians, but when the Emperor on his way to the
East appeared in Palestine, he promised them an am-
nesty if they would join his cause. This they did.
On his return he broke his pledge, the monks assuring
him of the divine pardon for this breach of faith, and
punished the Jews severely for their defection.

RELIGIOUS HISTORY OF THE ERA

The position of the patriarch remained hereditary
in the house of Judah Hanasi, until the office was abolished by the decree of Emperor Theodosius II (about
420). The successors of Judah Hanasi were Gamaliel

III, Judah II, Gamaliel IV, Judah III, Hillel II, Gamaliel V, Judah IV, and Gamaliel VI.   These patriarchs,
however, were not prominent as scholars, and while
they were the religious heads of the community, the
prerogatives of the president of the school of Tiberias
were transferred to a scholar of prominence.   Thus
Judah Hanasi himself appointed his son Gamaliel as
his successor before his death, but Rabbi Hanina was
named as president of the school.   It is probable that
the head of this school presided also over the court
sessions, so that he was the Ab Beth Din; the Nasi,
who formerly exercised these prerogatives, was the
representative of the Jewish community only through
the dignity of his office.

Prominent among the disciples of Hanina were
Johanan bar Nappaha, Simeon ben Lakish, and Eleazar
bar Padath (250–280).   Even at this period the Mishnah was already considered revealed law, which
the teacher could only explain, but not alter.   We
therefore very often find their names in the Talmud at the head of discussions of a passage in the
Mishnah.   They introduced the period of the Palestinian Amoraim, as the scholars following the era of
the Mishnah are called in contradistinction to the
teachers of the Mishnah, known as Tanaim.   To the
school of Johanan belong all prominent Palestinian
rabbis of the succeeding generation.   Prominent among
them is Abbahu of Cæsarea.   He is known not merely
as an expounder of the law but as a controversialist
against Christianity.

Tiberias continued to be the center of Jewish spiritual life, and quite a number of young scholars from
Babylonia came there to finish their studies; some of

them remained in Palestine. Of the teachers of the fourth century, little more than their names is known. Prominently mentioned, however, is Rabbi Jose, to whom is ascribed the final redaction of the Palestinian Talmud (350). At about this time Hillel II gave up the only tangible privilege of the Nasi, the announcement of the calendar. Instead of announcing the leap-year whenever it was necessary to postpone the Passover, fixed rules for the calendar were made. By this arrangement it became necessary to keep the second holydays, which had been celebrated in those places the messengers of the Nasi could not reach in time. Hillel ruled, however, that this practice had become hallowed by tradition, and that even henceforth the Jews living outside of Palestine should continue to celebrate two holydays.

When finally the office of patriarch was abolished, Palestine lost its place as the spiritual center of Judaism. The study of the law declined, and from the middle of the fourth century we find in Palestine studies confined to homiletical and exegetical works, due in part to the controversies with the Christians. Some of their greatest teachers, such as Jerome, the translator of the Bible into Latin, were disciples of Palestinian rabbis. Of the homiletical explanations collections were made; these are called Midrash. The oldest of these collections is the Midrash Rabba to Genesis, compiled in the seventh century.

BABYLONIA

Although in the fifth century B.C., Ezra is already mentioned as an expounder of the law, who had come from Babylon, although Hillel is said to have arrived in Palestine also from Babylon in the first century B.C. with a reputation for scholarship, and although Judah Hanasi is quoted as having said that the only man whose superiority he acknowledged was Huna, the Exilarch of Babylon, we find no distinct traces of literary activity in Babylon until the third century. At that time two men were prominent as scholars: Abba Areka, called Rab, and Samuel. Both had spent some time in Palestine, studying under Judah Hanasi. Rab was a member of the committee which assisted Judah Hanasi in the compilation of the Mishnah. Before he left Palestine, he was ordained by Judah Hanasi somewhat restrictedly, because it was a rule that the full prerogatives of the members of the Sanhedrin could not be exercised outside of the Holy Land. Probably for this reason Judah Hanasi refused to confer ordination upon Samuel. Rab taught in Sura, and Samuel in Nehardea. Both these places were for centuries the seats of prominent schools.

At this time, Rab was considered the greatest authority on ritual law, while Samuel was considered learned in civil law. Rab's decisions are characterized by rigorous interpretation of the law, especially as to Passover. Samuel accommodated himself more to the spirit of the times. From him we have the famous decision which makes the civil law of the country binding upon the Israelites as a religious obligation. He also partly abolished those laws of the Sabbatical year which had become obsolete, such as the cancellation of debts. He also declared that the celebration of the second holydays was unnecessary. He further laid down the principle that the Messianic prophecy merely meant the political independence of the Jews, and not a change in the condition of humanity.

To the next generation (250–300) belong Nahman bar Jacob, who reformed the legal procedure by introducing an oath in cases where formerly no oath had been necessary, Huna, Hisda, Shesheth and Judah bar Ezekiel, the last of whom was the founder of the new school of Pumbeditha, subsequently the most prominent of all Babylonian schools existing until the middle of the eleventh century. The characteristics of this age were the growth of dialecticism, Pilpul, and the neglect of Biblical studies. To the succeeding generation belong Rabba bar Nahmani and Rab Joseph. The latter is known as the author or compiler of the Aramaic translation of the prophets (Targum), more a paraphrase than a translation.

In the succeeding generation we have (350–380) Abaje and Raba, whose teachings are quoted as the most pronounced type of keen dialecticism. The most important of Babylonian Amoraim is Rab Ashe (350–431) who compiled the commentaries and the discourses on the Mishnah, and so became, with his successor Rabina (died 499), the compilers of the Babylonian Talmud. The successors of these teachers are called Saboraim (reasoners). Of their chronology and work we know nothing with exactness except that they lived during the sixth and in the early part of the seventh century. They arranged the subject-matter of the Talmud, which they divided into chapters and to which they added some explanatory remarks.

CHAPTER IV

FROM THE RISE OF ISLAM (622) TO THE ERA OF THE CRUSADES (1096)

Jews had been living in Arabia long before the time of Mohammed, perhaps as early as the pre-Christian era. Their mode of life was like that of the Arabs. They were divided into tribes, and had fortified places to which they retreated in case of feuds with their Arab neighbors. Like the Arabs they had their warriors, who were at the same time poets. A famous man from the time preceding Mohammed is Samuel ibn Adijah. He is known among the Arabs as a faithful friend, because when an Arab chieftain, one of his friends, sought refuge in his fortress, he allowed his son, who was in the hands of the enemy, to be killed rather than deliver the fugitive into their hands.

Mohammed had frequent intercourse with the Jews, and received from them the first impetus to found a new religion in place of the crude worship of the old Arabs. He laid particular stress on converting the Jews to the new religion, which was to be a universal theocracy. For this purpose he adopted some of the Jewish ideas, customs, and modes of worship, the strict monotheistic idea, the fast of Yom Kippur and the turning toward Jerusalem in prayer. The Jews, however, were offended at his sensuality, and ridiculed him for his ignorance. He therefore became

their enemy, and after the capture of one of their
forts, killed the inhabitants who had surrendered. All
other Jews were expelled from Arabia, which was to
be a theocratically governed state, where only the
religion of Mohammed would be tolerated.

Under Mohammed's successors, the Caliphs, Islam
rapidly spread over a great part of Asia and the theo-
cratic principle could not be maintained. Under
Omar (634–644), who conquered Jerusalem in 637, a
law called the Covenant of Omar governing the treatment of non-Mohammedans was proclaimed. By this
law the Jews had to pay a poll-tax, and were exempt
from military service. In spite of certain disabilities,
they enjoyed a relative state of freedom, and, as the
literature of the period proves, greeted the rise of
Islam as a relief from the oppression they had suffered
in Christian countries and in Persia. They also
looked upon Islam as the first step toward the reali-
zation of the Messianic kingdom. The improvement
of their condition was especially manifest in Spain,
which was conquered by the Mohammedans in 711.

GERMANIC NATIONS

Beginning with the fourth century, various Germanic tribes settled on the soil of the old Roman
Empire, and began to establish independent kingdoms
in the fifth century within its limits, until in 476 the
last Emperor, who was a ruler in name only, was
deposed. In Italy, where Theodoric had founded the
kingdom of the Ostrogoths in 493, the Jews were
fairly treated, although Theodoric, a fanatical Christian, considered the Jews an undesirable element. He
would, however, allow no injustice to be done them,

and when a mob in Ravenna destroyed a synagogue in 519, he ordered the city to make restitution; for this he was severely censured by Ambrosius, the Bishop of Milan. The Jews held the rule of the Goths to be preferable to that of the Byzantines, and in the war between these two powers, which ended with the overthrow of the Gothic kingdom (555) they aided the former, and their bravery in defending the city of Naples was highly praised by Greek historians.

After a short period of domination by the Byzantines, the Longobards, another German tribe, conquered Italy in 568. They do not seem to have taken any interest in the Jews, as their government was restricted to members of their own nationality. The Jews, as Roman citizens, were under the authority of the Roman government, which, as the Byzantines could not exercise any authority, was left almost entirely in the hands of the Bishop of Rome, the highest local dignitary. From the records of this period, we possess information as to the attitude of Pope Gregory I (590–604), in dealing with Jewish affairs. While naturally not in sympathy with the Jews, he insisted that they be treated fairly. Thus, he ordered that a cross, which a Jewish convert to Christianity had placed in a synagogue to spite the Jews, be removed, and when a synagogue had been converted into a church, he ordered an indemnity paid to its former owners. But he very often censured the Frankish kings for allowing the Jews to hold public offices and to keep Christian slaves.

FRANCE

The Merovingian kings who conquered Ancient Gaul in 496 were the first of the Germanic rulers to adopt the Roman Catholic religion. All the others were Arians. In the sixth century they treated the Jews kindly; we hear of a Jew named Priscus, a favorite of King Hilperic (561–584), whom that king loved so well that he wished him converted to Christianity. On one occasion Priscus discussed religious problems very freely in the presence of the King, with Bishop Gregory of Tours, and criticized Christian dogmas fearlessly. In spite of the representations of Pope Gregory I, the Frankish kings entrusted the Jews with offices, such as tax collector, and allowed them to deal in Christian slaves. Church councils, however, as early as the fifth century, legislated against social intercourse between Christians and Jews.

SPAIN

The Visigoths, who ruled over Spain, treated the Jews worse than any other nation at that time. All the mediæval disabilities, such as the seclusion of the Jews in certain quarters and the restriction of their worship, had their origin in that country. Frequently we hear of a law prohibiting the holding of Christian slaves by Jews. Repeatedly Jews were converted by force, and occasionally whole communities expelled. Bishop Isidore of Seville (560–630) wrote a book entitled "Against the Jews," which was widely read and translated into different languages. His example was imitated in later times. In the Frankish kingdom, Agobard, Archbishop of Lyons (814-840), wrote five books on the Jews, the titles of which show his animus: "On the Insolence of the Jews," "On the Necessity of Guarding Against Having Company with Jews," etc. He opposed the law which prohibited the

baptism of heathenish slaves owned by Jews and agi-
tated for their social seclusion. Similar was the literary activity of Amolo, Archbishop of Lyons (841–852),
who wrote a book against the Jews and dedicated it
to Emperor Charles III.

Charlemagne (768–814) is reported to have called
Kalonymus of Lucca to Mayence as chief rabbi of all
the Jews of Germany; but this report is legendary.
Equally unauthentic are laws ascribed to Charlemagne,
among them the one imposing upon the Jews an igno-
minious form of oath. A law of Charlemagne's son
Louis (814–840), required the markets to be held on
Sundays in order to make it possible for the Jews to
attend them.

The Jews in those days were chiefly traders, import-
ers of merchandise from foreign lands, and slave
dealers, and acted as the pioneers of commerce in the
countries of Western and Northern Europe.

LITERARY ACTIVITY OF THE PERIOD

The improvement in the condition of the Jews of
Spain, which began with the Arabic conquest of that
country in 711, made itself felt in their literary activity. Especially was this the case in the Caliphate
of Cordova, under Abderrahman (912–961). At his
court, Hasdai ibn Shaprut rose to prominence, and,
like the Mohammedan nobles of the time, gathered
around him a number of eminent authors and scholars. Among them were Menahem ben Saruk and
Dunash ibn Labrat, who first laid the foundation for
a scientific Hebrew grammar. Their disciples were
Judah Hayug and Mervan ibn Ganah, called Marinus.
The center of Jewish learning still remained in Baby-

lonia, where, after the conquest of the Persians by the
Mohammedans, a revival of learning took place.

The two principal schools were those of Sura and
Pumbeditha, and at the head of each was a president,
ריש מתיבתא. The one at Sura was the higher in rank,
and was called Gaon (excellency), a title which later
was transferred to the president of the school in Pumbeditha. The function of the Gaon was to preside over
the regular course of studies, Sidra, and the popular
extension course called Kalla, held twice a year in the
months preceding the Passover and the fall festivals.
He further rendered decisions in important cases submitted to him from all parts of the world. A number of collections of these decisions called Teshubot
(Responsa), have come down to us. They are written
partly in Aramaic and partly in Arabic, according to
the language in which the question was written.

The Gaon licensed rabbis, or judges, as they were
called, because their chief function was to act as
judges in civil cases. These licenses were endorsed
by the Exilarch, Resh Galutha, the political head of
the communities in Babylonia, representing them before the government and appointing the Gaon. The
former, in turn, was appointed by the Caliph, and his
office was hereditary as a rule. The oldest literary
works of the period are collections of laws regarding
matters of frequent occurrence, such as liturgy,
mourning, the reception of proselytes, etc. They are
known as the "Small Tractates," and are usually
found in the ninth volume of our editions of the
Talmud.

Other compendia of the law are the Halakot Gedo-
lot by Simeon Kayara, written in the eighth century,

and the Sheeltot of Ahai of Shabha, the latter arranged according to the Pentateuch, and containing some moral lessons besides the legal exposition of the text. The compilation of these works was opposed by the Gaonim, who considered them injurious to the study of the law and detrimental to their own authority.

In the ninth century the first Talmudic dictionary ערוך was written by Zemah Gaon. His work has not come down to us, but most of it was incorporated in the Talmudic dictionary of the same name, written by Nathan of Rome in the eleventh century. The title has also been retained by subsequent compilers of Talmudic dictionaries, including the Aruch Completum, edited by Alexander Kohut (1878–1892). At the same time Amram Gaon compiled the first liturgy, Seder Rab Amram, and thus is the originator of our present prayer-book. The form in which this compilation has come down to us is not as the original left the hands of its editor, for quite a number of later texts are found in it and its order of services is not exactly identical with any of the rituals in use at present. Still, it is the groundwork of the liturgy of Judaism to-day all over the world.

From the same period dates, probably, the first Kabalistic book which we possess, the "Sefer Yezirah" (Book of Creation). It may be called a theosophical treatise, written in the language and form of the Mishnah, and based on the philosophy of the Pythagorean and Alexandrian schools. Its subject-matter naturally makes it obscure; from the tenth century at least it has been commented upon. Legend has ascribed its authorship to Rabbi Akiba, and even to Biblical persons such as Abraham.

In the ninth century we meet the first traces of a
scientific literature. Prominent here is Saadya Gaon
(892–942), born in Fayum, and called to Sura as
Gaon, quite an unusual event. His literary activity
extends over the whole field of Jewish literature. He
wrote commentaries on the Bible besides an Arabic
translation, and on Talmudic topics. He also composed religious hymns, but the most important of all
his works is his אמונות ודעות (Dogma and Science), the
first attempt at a scientific apology for Judaism from
a philosophical point of view. His independence
brought him into conflict with the Exilarch David ben
Zakkai, to whose dictates he would not submit in a
matter which he regarded as unjust; consequently he
was deposed. Saadya contended that this act was
illegal and excommunicated the Exilarch. The latter
proved stronger and Saadya was forced into exile.
Later on, however, they became reconciled, and
Saadya was reinstated (934).

The last two Gaonim of any importance lived in
Pumbeditha. They were Sherira, who died in 999,
and his son, Hay Gaon, who died in 1038. From the
former we possess a very important historical treatise
on the development of Rabbinic law known as the
epistle of Sherira Gaon. It was written at the request
of a man in Morocco, and was inspired by apologetic
motives to prove that the law had been handed down
unaltered from generation to generation. From Hay
Gaon we have various Talmudic works, many responsa,
and a didactic poem. Their contemporary was Samuel
ibn Hofni, a rationalistic writer, who rejected the belief in the miracles related in the Talmud. Otherwise
the age of the Gaonim is characterized by a blind faith,

not only in Bible and Talmud, but also in popular superstitions and in the preservation of superstitious customs.   Hay was succeeded by Hezekiah, who after holding his office for two years was put to death by the Caliph in 1040.   After this time the office lost all significance.   Names of a few of those who held office after this time are found, but nothing is known of their activity, nor has any literary work of this age come down to us.

The blind faith which characterized the period of the Gaonim aroused considerable opposition, culminating in the foundation of a religious sect called the Karaites, בני מקרא, ''Sons of the Bible.''   Their founder was Anan ben David (760) who claimed the Bible as the only authority for faith and practice, and therefore rejected all Rabbinic law.   His successors founded a congregation in Jerusalem, and very soon spread in the East.   The most prominent teachers of the Karaites are Benjamin of Nehawend, and Salman ben Jeroham, the latter of whom carried on a literary controversy with Saadya.   Judah Hadassi, in the thirteenth century wrote אשכל הכפר, the standard work of the Karaite law, written in rhymed prose.   Other important Karaite scholars are Aaron ben Elijah, who died in 1369, the author of גן עדן, a compendium of the religious law, and עץ חיים, a work on religious philosophy.

In the fifteenth century Elijah Bashjazi wrote another compendium of the Karaite religion entitled אדרת אליהו.   By this period a large Karaite community settled in Lithuania, where Isaac of Troki wrote a very able polemical treatise directed against Christianity, known as חזוק אמונה.   In 1698, Jacob Trigland,

professor at Leyden, made inquiries concerning the
Karaites by means of a letter addressed to their chief
sent through an ambassador to Poland. He received
a reply, דודמרדכי, written by Mordecai ben Nissim.
This was, for a long time, the only source of information on the history of the Karaites. The last Karaite
author of any consequence was Abraham Firkovitch
(1787–1874) of Russia, who discovered and published
important Karaite documents. Some of these, however, he forged in the interest of the Karaite claim
that the Karaites represent the original Judaism from
which the Rabbanites seceded.

At the same time that the Karaite schism occurred,
the Chazars, a Tartar tribe, were converted to Judaism.
Reports of the existence of a Jewish kingdom had
reached the Jews of Western Europe. Hasdai ibn
Shaprut wrote a letter of inquiry on this. He received
a reply from the King of the Chazars, and these two
letters are the chief source of information concerning
this remarkable event. Toward the end of the tenth
century the kingdom of the Chazars was conquered by
the Russians. Judah Halevi, who wrote his Kuzari
about 1140, used the story of the conversion of the
Chazar King in the form of a philosophic dialogue between him and the rabbi who converted him. The
knowledge he had of an independent Jewish state was
the basis of the fanciful reports circulated by an
adventurer who called himself Eldad Hadani and
pretended to be a descendant of one of the lost ten
tribes. Their habitation and modes of life he de-
scribed in a book. He appeared in the tenth century
in Morocco, but nothing is known as to what finally
became of him.

In the ninth century, the literature of religious hymns, Piyut, begins. The authors of these are called Payetanim (poets). Their works are characterized by arbitrary handling of the Hebrew grammar, by the creation of new words in an arbitrary style, and finally, by obscure allusions to the Midrash. The oldest of these poets are Jose ben Jose and Jannai. Their successor, Eleazar ben Kallir, is the most prolific of all. Of his life we know nothing with certainty.

The literary activity of the Jews of Europe began in the ninth century. The first work is probably the Josippon, a history of the Jews from the [destruction of Babylon by Cyrus to the downfall of Jerusalem in 70, which was ascribed to Josephus Flavius. Another anonymous writer, who lived in Italy in the ninth century, is the author of the Midrash, called Pirke Rabbi Eliezer. But the first Jewish author who lived in Europe, known by name, is Sabbatai Donolo (913–982), who wrote on medicine, astrology, and Kabbala.

CHAPTER V

THE JEWS OF EUROPE (1040–1215)

THE first mention of Jews in Germany is found in two orders of Emperor Constantine (321), in which he regulated the condition of the Jews of Cologne. It is possible that this settlement was of a temporary character, for nothing is heard of the Jews in Germany until the tenth century. A statement to the effect that Charlemagne called Rabbi Kalonymus of Lucca in Italy to be Chief Rabbi of all the Jews of Germany is first reported in the sixteenth century, and is in all likelihood legendary. Under Charlemagne the Jews appear in Germany only as travelling traders. In 1016, however, there was already a bloody persecution of the Jews in Mayence. Gershom ben Judah, a native of France, was rabbi in Mayence. He occupied so prominent a position that he was called מאור הגולה (light of the exile). He wrote commentaries on various parts of the Talmud, responsa, other Talmudic works, and liturgical poetry. He died in 1028. To him are ascribed various rules, among them a prohibition of polygamy and an injunction to respect the secrecy of letters. At the same time there lived in Mayence Simeon bar Isaac, the liturgical poet, whose hymns are found in the ritual of the German Jews for the second day of Rosh Hashana.

In 1090 Emperor Henry IV granted charters to the Jews of Worms and Speyer. These are the oldest laws regulating the status of the Jews in Germany, granting to them freedom of trade and travel, proclaiming the inviolability of their cemeteries, and prohibiting the kidnapping and baptism of their children. Six years later the first crusade broke out, and the mobs composing the army of the crusaders on the Rhine invaded the Jewish settlements, chiefly Cologne, Mayence, Speyer and Worms, in that part of the country. Houses were sacked, synagogues desecrated, and many Jews cruelly murdered; others committed suicide after killing their own children in order to save them from forced conversions. A number of Jews who had been converted to Christianity, in order to save their lives, later on returned to Judaism in spite of the ecclesiastic law which put this under the penalty of death. The Emperor, who at that time was in Italy, sanctioned this in spite of the protests of the Pope.

Another persecution broke out in 1146, when the second crusade began. But the consequences were not as serious as those of the first crusade. Bernard of Clairvaux strongly condemned all acts of violence toward the Jews, who found refuge in the castles of the lords, and the Bishop of Speyer opened his castle, the Wolkenburg, to them, protecting them from the attacks of the mob. Still, in Wuerzburg, quite a number were killed, under the charge of having murdered a Christian. This may be considered the first blood-accusation on the European continent, although no particular motive for the crime was given. There is, however, a case on record in England in 1144, where the Jews were accused of having murdered a boy, William of Norwich, and nailed him to a cross in order to mock the crucifixion of Jesus.

During the course of the twelfth century, local outbreaks of mob violence occurred everywhere in Europe, notably at Blois, France, in 1171, where thirty-four Jews were burned at the stake.   In 1189, on the occasion of the coronation of King Richard Cœur de Lion, a bloody persecution took place in London, and soon spread over the other cities of the kingdom. Notable is the case of Benedict of York, who, in order to save his life, turned to Christianity and returned to Judaism on the next day.   Both King Richard and the Archbishop of Canterbury permitted this, although it was against the canonical law.

The climax of the ill-treatment of the Jews was reached in 1215, when the Lateran Council, presided over by Pope Innocent III, passed various laws repeating the usual prohibition against office-holding by Jews, and decreeing that they should wear a distinct mark on their outer garments.   This is the origin of the Yellow Badge, which in some countries continued to be in force until the end of the eighteenth century. The Pope stated that the Jews should be like Cain, singled out for their wickedness, and that their treatment should be an object lesson to Christians.

SPIRITUAL LIFE OF THE PERIOD

The spiritual life of the Jews reached its highest development in Spain, where the contact with the cultured Arabs, whose language the Jews spoke, made the works of the ancient Greek philosophers and scientists accessible to them.   In the beginning of the eleventh century Bahya ibn Pakuda, a philosopher, wrote "The Duties of the Heart," perhaps the most popular work of this literature.   His ideal of life is asceticism.

His contemporary, Solomon ibn Gabirol (born 1022), wrote a philosophical book, "The Fountain of Life," which, however, is only extant in a Latin translation. He also wrote an ethical treatise, "The Choicest of Pearls," and some Hebrew poetry. His poems, of which quite a number have found place in the liturgy, are among the best works of their class. Of his secular poems in Hebrew, a wine song is the most famous. About the same time Samuel Hanagid was secretary to the King of Granada. He was not only a patron of Jewish learning but an author of considerable note. He wrote an introduction to the Talmud, and various works which are sequels to Biblical books, such as Psalms, Proverbs, and Ecclesiastes. His son, Joseph, succeeded him, and was killed in a riot in 1060.

The greatest Hebrew poet of mediæval times is Judah Halevi (born about 1080, died 1141). Of his numerous poems, some are of a religious, others of a secular character. Of the latter the best known is a description of a sea voyage; of the former, the Ode to Zion, embodied in the ritual for the ninth of Ab and translated into various modern languages. He also wrote an apology for Judaism, called Kuzari, previously mentioned, which presents its doctrines in the form of dialogues between the King of the Chazars and the rabbi who converted him. In 1140 he went to Palestine to spend the remainder of his days there. He seems to have died before he reached his goal. A younger contemporary is Abraham ibn Ezra (1092–1167). He was born in Spain, and travelled through a great part of Europe and the Orient. Of his numerous works, comprising the fields of poetry, Hebrew

grammar, astrology, and other subjects, the most note-
worthy is his commentary on the Pentateuch, which
makes him rank as the first Biblical critic. He proved
by his strong critical arguments that the Pentateuch
as we possess it does not come from Moses but was
partly the product of later times. His contemporary
is Moses ibn Ezra, a very prolific Hebrew poet, whose
poems, however, suffer from an excessive play on
words. It is not known whether the two Ibn Ezras
were relatives.

The most illustrious author of mediæval times is
Moses ben Maimon (Maimonides, born at Cordova,
1135; died at Cairo, 1204). His first work was a
commentary on the Mishnah, written in Arabic, and
translated into Hebrew by Samuel ibn Tibbon. This
work was a preparation for the greatest work of his
life, the "Mishneh Torah," in which he presents the
whole doctrine and law of Judaism. It is written in
clear Hebrew, and, while in the law following the Rabbinic sources, it shows here and there, especially in
the dogmatic part, the author's object to harmonize
Judaism with philosophical thought. He is the author
of a philosophic work, "The Guide of the Perplexed,"
written in Arabic and known by its Hebrew title,
Moreh Nebukim. His object of harmonizing religion
with philosophy is made manifest in the first part of
this work by his attempt to explain the anthropomor-
phic passages of the Bible. He also explains prophecy
as a divine gift and tries to present reasons for the
divine laws, showing that they are intended for the
instruction and the material and moral elevation of
mankind. The book was translated into Hebrew by
Samuel ibn Tibbon in the twelfth century, and by

Judah Alcharizi in the thirteenth.   It was at an early
date translated into Latin, and in recent times into
various modern languages.   Maimonides in addition
wrote quite a number of works on scientific subjects,
notably on medicine, and various Rabbinic works.
He was physician in ordinary to the Sultan.

Of the Talmudists of this period, the greatest is Solomon ben Isaac (Rashi) of Troyes (1040–1105).   He
wrote a commentary on almost the whole Babylonian
Talmud printed in all Talmuds, and a standard work
to-day.   He is the author of commentaries on most of
the Biblical books.   His commentary on the Pentateuch contains in clear and concise language the Rabbinic interpretation of the Mosaic law and well-chosen
homiletical interpretations from the Midrash, and is
one of the most popular works in the Rabbinic literature.   It has been printed with the text of the
Pentateuch innumerable times, and is a very popular
text-book in Jewish study circles all over the world.
Rashi wrote other Rabbinic works and religious
hymns.   The most prominent Rabbinic author of this
period in Spain was Isaac Alfasi (born in Fez, 1013;
died in Spain, 1103).   He wrote an abridged Talmud,
omitting all discussions of matters not of legal interest and all the laws not in force after the destruction
of the Temple.   By this method he facilitated the ren-
dering of legal decisions.   In Italy there lived at this
time Nathan ben Jehiel of Rome, who wrote a Talmud dictionary "Aruk," using the work of the same
title by Zemach Gaon.

Rashi's grandsons, Samuel, Isaac and Jacob ben
Meir were also prominent Talmudic authors.   Samuel
ben Meir (Rashbam) wrote several Talmudic treatises,

supplements to his grandfather's commentaries, and a commentary on the Pentateuch somewhat more free from the blind, unrestricted submission to Rabbinic authority which characterizes his grandfather's work. The greatest Talmudist among the brothers was Jacob ben Meir (Rabbenu Tam, died 1171), whose chief work is "Sefer Hayashar," in which he proclaims the principle that the contradictions in the Talmud must be harmonized. These men are the founders of a school of authors known as Tosafists, from "Tosafot" (Additions), glosses to Rashi's Talmud commentary. These glosses are printed in most of our editions of the Talmud. Through the activities of these men the French province of Champagne and Western Germany became the chief seats of Rabbinic studies.

CHAPTER VI

PERIOD OF OPPRESSION (1215-1492)

DURING the thirteenth century the persecutions of the Jews continued, although they are of a more sporadic character than those of the time of the crusades. In 1235 a number of Jews were killed in Fulda on the charge of ritual murder. This is the first distinct case of its kind, but was frequently repeated in France and various places in Germany, although Emperor Frederick II (1236) and Pope Innocent IV (1247) defended the Jews against this accusation.

An important change in the political condition of the Jews resulted from the law of Frederick the Belligerent of Austria (1244). In this law the territorial ruler for the first time proclaimed his right to legislate for the Jews, heretofore considered the exclusive privilege of the Emperor of Germany, as overlord of all the Jews. This law deals largely with the regulation of money-lending. It permits a very high rate of interest, and allows the Jews to be tried in accordance with their own laws. It prohibits all violence toward the persons and properties of the Jews, their synagogues and cemeteries, and forbids the forcible baptism of Jewish children. It became the prototype for all similar mediæval legislation, and was repeated almost verbatim in subsequent laws issued by the kings of Bohemia, Hungary, the Dukes of Saxony and Silesia, and others during the thirteenth century.

In England, the Jews were constantly being black-
mailed by King John (1199–1216) and by King Henry
III (1216–1272). The most notable and typical instance of the extortion of money from the Jews, is
that reported of King John, who imprisoned a Jew
and ordered that one of his teeth should be drawn
every day until he agreed to pay the sum demanded of
him. The heavy taxes laid upon the Jews forced
them to charge higher rates of interest, thus embitter-
ing the people against them, and making them so
miserable that they asked to be permitted to emigrate.
Finally Edward I, in 1290, ordered the expulsion of all
the Jews from England. They were permitted to take
their property with them, and a sea captain, who put
the Jewish exiles aboard his vessel on a sand bar
where they were drowned by the high tide, was put to
death.

In France the vassals possessed power independent
of the crown. There the Jews were expelled from the
territory of the king and recalled several times during
the fourteenth century. At each expulsion they were
robbed, so that an assembly of Jewish notables proposed to declare it unlawful, under penalty of excom-
munication, for any Jew to settle in territory from
which the Jews had been previously expelled. Judah
Hechasid, author of a book on religious ethics, however, condemned this resolution because it would not
be effective and merely cause the Jews to transgress
the law.

A very serious persecution broke out in Franconia,
in 1298, the Jews being accused of desecrating the
host in Roettingen. This is the first case of this kind,
often repeated up to the sixteenth century. The

leader of the mob was a man named Rindfleisch. Another bloody persecution broke out in Alsace, in 1336, under the leadership of an innkeeper, John Arm-leder, so called because he fastened to his arm a patch of leather which was imitated by all his followers. These riots were finally suppressed after having brought great misery upon the Jews, but the evil-doers were not punished.

The most serious persecutions broke out in 1348–1349, during the so-called Black Plague which spread all over Europe. As a reason for these attacks the rumor was circulated that the Jews had poisoned the wells or had smeared some poisonous salve on the doors. In many cases the Jews were killed and their houses sacked. The protection of the Emperor availed them nothing; even if the Emperor threatened a city with punishment for breach of the peace, the affair was usually compromised by allowing the city to retain part of the plunder taken from the Jews, the Emperor taking the rest. The Flagellants, who ap-peared at about this time, by their religious fanati-cism also stimulated the hatred against the Jews.

Other annoyances were frequent. On the basis of the view that the Jews were chattels of the king, various rulers occasionally declared void the bonds held by the Jews. The most typical instance is that of Wenzel, King of Bohemia and German Emperor, who in 1385 annulled all the bonds held by Jews and accepted from the debtors a fraction of their debts in settlement.

During the fifteenth century frequent expulsions took place. The cities, originally small settlements where the Jews were the merchants and bankers, had grown in size and importance, and the citizens were jealous of their successful Jewish competitors. Such expulsions were often ordered under the excitement aroused by some false accusation. Thus, in 1421, the Jews of Vienna were accused of having desecrated the host, and a number of them were publicly burned at the stake, all the others being expelled from the city and the entire province. Such expulsions took place in 1426 at Cologne, the oldest Jewish settlement in Germany, in 1440, at Wittenberg, and in 1475 at Bamberg.

The religious troubles of this period contributed to turn the people against the Jews. The Hussites were then a great menace to the Church, and John Capistrano, an Italian monk, preached against them in various places in the kingdom of Bohemia. Everywhere he set the mob against the Jews, and occasionally as at Breslau in 1453, he tried them on the charge of ritual murder. A number of Jews were burned at the stake, and many others expelled. From other cities of that kingdom, as Bruenn and Olmuetz, the Jews were expelled.

Another Catholic revivalist, Bernardin of Feltre, appeared in Trent, where he arranged a ritual murder trial. The body of a boy named Simon was found, and the Jews were accused of having murdered him (1475). Again a number of Jews were cruelly put to death and the remainder expelled in spite of the fact that the Doge of Venice exonerated them from the charge, and that the Pope declared the accusation to be baseless. Simon was considered a martyr and later on made a saint. A similar charge was brought against the Jews of Ratisbon, but they succeeded in

proving their innocence. The expulsions continued. In 1499 the Jews were expelled from Nuremberg and Ulm, in 1493 from Magdeburg, in 1496 from the province of Styria, and somewhat later from Ratisbon and Saxony. The exiles sought refuge in villages and little towns under the rule of the nobles, or emigrated to Poland, where, toward the end of the fifteenth century, there was already a considerable Jewish settlement. This soon became in numbers the most important in Europe.

FRANCE

Under Louis IX (1226–1270), a religious fanatic, the Jews were treated badly. In 1236 a mob of crusaders attacked them, and wrought great suffering among them. In 1240 Nicholas Donin, a converted Jew, brought charges against the Talmud as containing statements which were blasphemous to the Christian religion. Consequently all copies that could be found were seized and in cart-loads were publicly burnt at Paris in 1244. In 1254 the King decreed the expulsion of all the Jews from France, but the decree was repealed under Philip IV (1288–1314). All the Jews found in the kingdom were imprisoned and their property confiscated under Philip's successor, Louis X. They were recalled in 1315, but under Philip V suffered greatly from a fanatical mob, known as Shepherd Crusaders. After many vicissitudes their final expulsion was decreed in 1394. Only in the south of France, where the feudal barons still had sovereign rights, and in the Papal possessions at Carpentras and Avignon, a few isolated Jewish communities, with a ritual of their own, remained. Most of the Jews exiled

from France went to the adjoining German territories
of Alsace and Lorraine, and when these territories
were annexed to France in the sixteenth and seventeenth centuries, the Jews were permitted to remain
there. But they were not allowed to settle in France
proper until 1791.

SPAIN

The Christian kingdoms in the latter part of the
Middle Ages continually expanded, so that the Moors
were restricted to the southern part of the peninsula.
The growing religious fanaticism of the Christians
affected the condition of the Jews unfavorably, but
individuals rose to prominence as financiers or physicians. James VIII of Aragon ordered a public disputation between Jews and Christians held at Barcelona
in 1263. The Jewish side was defended by Moses
ben Nachman, and, although he had been assured perfect freedom of speech, the Christians took such offence
at his remarks that they demanded his execution.
The King sent him instead into exile. He went to
Palestine, where he died. Alphonso X (1254-1284),
of Castile, employed Don Isaac, a Jew, as his astronomer. Alphonso's constitution, regulating the condition of the Jews, is rather severe. They were restricted
in their commercial activity and compelled to wear
yellow badges.

In a civil war between Peter the Cruel (1350-1369)
and Henry II (1369-1379) the Jews sided with the
former, and although Henry was victorious he treated
them with moderation. In 1391 Ferdinand Martinez
began to preach violent sermons against the Jews in
Toledo, the largest Jewish community of Spain. His

example was followed in many other places, and in consequence of these incendiary speeches, riots broke out all over Christian Spain. A great many Jews were killed or forcibly converted to Christianity. Many of the latter fled as soon as they were able to do so to Mohammedan countries in order to be able to practice the Jewish religion openly. They were called Marannos, probably from the Hebrew מוחרם (excommunicated). The Jews called them אנוסים (compelled to profess the Christian religion).

In 1413–1414 another public disputation between Jews and Christians was arranged by Pope Benedict XIII, one of the three who claimed the Papal throne at that time. It took place in Tortosa, Aragon. The idea had been suggested to the Pope by Solomon Halevi, a converted Jew who called himself Paul and later on became Bishop of Burgos. He was an influential friend of the King of Castile. Another convert, a Jewish scholar like Paul, had written a satire against Paul and his conversion. This was Joshua Alorqui, who as a Christian took the name of Geronimo de Santa Fe, and was derisively called by the Jews מגד"ף, "Blasphemer."

Among those who took up the cudgels for the Jews at Tortosa was Joseph Albo, author of the philosophic work "Ikkarim." The many converts whom the Church forced to remain [in her fold while they were Jews at heart and secretly practiced Judaism, provoked the ecclesiastic authorities. For their sake a special court of inquiry, called the "Inquisition," was created in 1480. This may be defined as a court-martial to try cases of heresy. It proceeded with the utmost severity and with absolute disregard of the most elementary forms of court procedure. From time to time it arranged public executions, at which those convicted of heresy were burned at the stake, often after having undergone terrible tortures. Such an execution was called an auto-da-fe.

In 1483 Thomas Torquemada was appointed Grand Inquisitor, and he was assisted by the blind monk, Peter Arbues. During the time of the existence of the Inquisition (1480–1808), 31,712 were burned at the stake and hundreds of thousands were punished with imprisonment, confiscation of property, or were publicly disgraced. One of the latter kinds of punishment was the sentence compelling the victim to wear a hideous penitential gown, the San Benito. Peter Arbues was assassinated by Marannos, and Pope Pius IX declared him a saint in 1868. The victims of the Inquisition were mostly converted Jews, although there were also Moors and native Christians among them. In spite of the terrors of the Inquisition, the Jews assisted the Marannos in the observance of the Jewish religion, and this was the cause of the edict of expulsion promulgated by Ferdinand, King of Castile, and his wife Isabella, Queen of Aragon, on March 30, 1492, soon after the capture of Granada, the last Moorish stronghold in Spain.

Most of the exiled fled to Portugal, where they found a temporary home. But when Manuel, King of Portugal, married the daughter of Ferdinand and Isabella, it was stipulated in the marriage contract that the Jews should be expelled from that country also. This expulsion took place in 1498. Most of the exiles went to Turkey, where they were kindly received. Others went to the Barbary States in Northern Africa, and especially to Morocco. A number went to Italy and settled in the various cities, even in the Papal possessions. Still there were a great many Marannos left in Spain, and while they were compelled to profess and practice the Catholic religion, they remained Jews for many generations. Hence up to the end of the eighteenth century, they were always autos-da-fe held at which Jews were publicly burned. From time to time the wealthy Marannos would escape and seek refuge in countries where they were permitted to publicly practice their religion.

ITALY

Italy was split up into many petty states whose boundary lines were constantly shifting. The treatment of the Jews varied in its details according to time and locality but is the same in general throughout mediæval times. It was characterized by restriction of economic liberty and humiliation in social position. The Jews produced quite a number of eminent scholars, physicians (sometimes attending on the Popes), astronomers and translators of Arabic works into Latin. Their economic activity was largely confined to money-lending and, in the fourteenth century, they became the pioneers of banking by combining the pawn-shops in a certain city into companies which were given the exclusive privilege of money-lending.

In the fifteenth century clerical agitation became very strong, and loan associations were formed under priestly management to suppress money-lending by Jews. One of the most notable agitators in this respect was Bernardin of Feltre, who is known through his participation in the ritual murder trial at Trent

(1475).   Italy became a force in Jewish culture by the establishment of the first Hebrew printing presses. The first book printed seems to have been published in 1474.   One of the earliest printed books was the "Psalms" with the commentary of David Kimhi, 1475.   The edict of the expulsion of the Jews from Spain affected also those of Sicily and southern Italy, at that time Spanish dependencies.   Since that period there has existed no Jewish community in that part of Italy.

HUNGARY

In Hungary the Jews settled at a very early date. They were tax-farmers and financiers.   Our first documentary evidence goes back to 1251, when King Bela IV granted them a charter, essentially a reproduction of that granted by the Duke of Austria in 1244.   Under Louis (1342–1382) they were given the alternative of expulsion or conversion to Christianity. During the fifteenth century the Jews suffered from persecution and expulsion.

POLAND

In Poland the Jews appear in the thirteenth century as a small community without any intellectual life. In 1264 they obtained their first charter, this being confirmed by Casimir the Great (1333–1370).   It is also a reproduction of the Austrian law of 1244. When Capistrano appeared (1450) in Poland the Jews suffered from mob attacks but fared not as badly as those of Bohemia.   The persecution of the Jews in Western Europe, beginning with the crusades, drove many of them to emigrate to the large and thinly settled kingdom of Poland.   Hence toward the close of the fifteenth century, Poland was the center of Rabbinic learning and has to-day proportionately the largest Jewish population in the world.

THE EAST

In 1187 Saladin reconquered Jerusalem. From that time Jews began to emigrate to Palestine and Egypt. The persecution of the Jews through the Inquisition and their expulsion from Spain drove many to Morocco and Algeria. The conquest of Constantinople by the Turks in 1453 brought many Jews to the Balkans, and the number of the immigrants was so large that their dialect, Ladino, became the universal language of the Jews of the East, just as in Poland and Hungary the immigrants from Germany made Yiddish predominant.

JEWISH LITERATURE,
THIRTEENTH TO FIFTEENTH CENTURY

From the thirteenth century the spiritual life of the Jews declined. Talmudic literature, ritualism and Kabbala were almost exclusively cultivated. Poetry, exegesis, philosophy and scientific literature were constantly declining. The most prominent representative of Maimonides' tradition is David Kimhi of Narbonne, 1170–1230. He wrote a Hebrew Grammar, מכלול, and commentaries to most of the Biblical books. He also took an active part in the defense of Maimonides' works when the orthodox of Spain and France, influenced by the zeal of the Dominican Friars in their attack on the Albigenses and the scholastic philosophy, wished to commit the "Moreh" to the flames. Besides Kimhi two members of his family are noted for grammatical and exegetical works. These are his father Joseph and his brother Moses. To Southern France belongs also the family of Ibn Tibbon, four generations of which were prominent translators of philosophical, Rabbinic and scientific books from Arabic into Hebrew.

Judah the Elder (1100–1150) translated Bahya's "Duties of the Heart," Saadya's "Dogma and Science," and Judah Halevi's "Kuzari." His son Solomon translated Maimonides' "Moreh" and the commentary on the Mishna. But the orthodox party prevailed in their opposition to Maimonides, and in 1233 the "Moreh" was publicly burned at Paris. The Dominicans, who had been appealed to, extended their inquisitory activities, and on the testimony of Nicholas Donin, a converted Jew, charged the Talmud with hostility to the Christians. All copies of the book that could be found were burned at Paris in 1244. In spite of these attacks philosophical studies did not die out completely. In the fourteenth century Levi ben Gershom (1288–1344) flourished in Southern France. His philosophical work, "The Wars of the Lord," is an attempt to reconcile Judaism with Platonic philosophy. He also invented an astronomic instrument in which the great astronomer Kepler was much interested.

To the fourteenth century belongs Hasdai Crescas, whose commentary to Maimonides' "Moreh" and philosophical treatise, "The Light of the Lord," have great scientific value. Of little independent value is the work "Ikkarim" (Fundamental Principles), by Joseph Albo (1380–1440). He is an imitator of Maimonides; but, instead of thirteen fundamental articles of faith, he recognized only three—God, revelation

and the future life. To the school of the preachers
belongs Isaac Arama, whose work, "Akedat Yizhak,"
is a philosophical interpretation of the Midrash, and
follows the weekly portions of the Haggadic writers.

Isaac Abarbanel, born in Lisbon, 1447, died in
Venice, 1508, wrote various dogmatic treatises in
which, as in his commentaries on the Pentateuch, he
outlined his views. He showed little independence,
sometimes plagiarized, and is very verbose. He put
together a great number of questions on some topic in
Biblical literature, and attempted to answer them.
From this time philosophy and scientific literature are
on the decline. The intellectual activity of the Jews
is confined mostly to Rabbinic literature.

Secular subjects are rarely taken up until the end
of the eighteenth century. Then a revival of secular
knowledge and scientific literature took place. Of
the scientific writers Jacob Anatoli, 1200–1250, in
Italy, translated serious scientific works from Arabic
and Hebrew into Latin for Frederick II. Kalonymos
ben Kalonymos of Rome, 1280–1340, wrote an ethical
treatise, "Eben Bohan" (Tried Stone from Isaiah
xxviii, 16), and a travesty on the Talmud, "Masseket
Purim." To the same period belong Immanuel ben
Solomon of Rome, a friend of Dante, author of
"Mehabberot," a poem in the style of the "Divina
Commedia." This in some places is lascivious, and
was condemned by Joseph Caro in the "Shulhan
Aruk." In the style of Dante, Moses Rieti (1388–
1460) wrote his "Mikdash Meat."

To the fifteenth century belong Judah Messer Leon
of Mantua, who wrote a text-book on rhetoric in
Hebrew, Nofet Zufim (honeycombs), and Elijah del

Medigo, a native of Crete, who was professor of philosophy in Padua. He wrote an apology for Judaism in Hebrew, "Behinat Ha-Dat" (Evidenced Religion). In this class the polemical writers against Christianity are included. Joshua Allorqui of Spain, who later on became a convert to Christianity, wrote such a polemical treatise under the title "Be not like thy fathers." In scientific literature we have the anthology of the Midrashim called "Yalkut Shimeoni," by Simeon Kara (the Bible reader) of the thirteenth century. This is a selection of homiletical expositions from old Rabbinic works arranged in the order of the books of the Bible. A similar work is the "Yalkut Machiri" of uncertain date, but most likely from the fourteenth century, by Machir ben Aba Mari. Only parts of it are in existence.

TALMUDIC LITERATURE

In the beginning of the thirteenth century, orthodox authorities in France and Spain attacked Maimonides' philosophy. Their leaders were Meir Abulafia in Spain, and Solomon ben Abraham of Montpellier in France. They denounced the work of Maimonides to the Dominicans, and the latter burned it publicly at Paris in 1244. Of Talmudic authorities who possessed secular learning and worked in the field of exegesis the most prominent was Moses ben Nachman of Gerona (Ramban, 1200–1270). His commentary on the Pentateuch contains sound exegetical views, is strictly traditional and gives space to Kabalistic interpretations. He indulged in vehement invectives against Ibn Ezra, and in his notes on Alfasi vehemently attacked Zerahiah Halevi for his critical remarks on Alfasi in "The Wars of the Lord."

One of the most prominent Spanish Rabbis was Solomon Ibn Adret (Rashba), in the thirteenth and fourteenth centuries. He was opposed to philosophy and issued a prohibition that no one should read the Moreh before he was twenty-five years old. He professed a belief in every statement in the Talmud, even if in conflict with well-known scientific facts. He left thousands of responsa.

A younger contemporary of his is Asher ben Yechiel, a disciple of Meir of Rothenburg (German rabbi of the thirteenth century), who emigrated to Spain in 1305 and died in Toledo in 1327. He wrote a work on the plan of that by Alfasi, making an abstract of the practical laws of the Talmud. It is printed in most of the Talmud editions, and quoted as Rosh. He had eight sons who were Talmudic scholars, and of these the most prominent was Jacob ben Asher, who died in 1350. He wrote an important set of codes of the Rabbinic law, called Turim. The first, Orah Hayyim, treated chiefly of liturgics, the second, Eben Haezer, of matrimonial laws, the third, Yoreh Deah, of dietary laws, the fourth, Hoshen Mishpat, of civil laws.

Another disciple of Meir of Rothenburg was Mordecai ben Hillel, who was killed in Nuremberg during the Rindfleisch riots of 1298. He wrote notes to Alfasi's code of value, because of their many historical references. To the fourteenth century belongs Isaac ben Sheshet (Ribash) of Barcelona, who fled after the persecution of 1391, and became Chief Rabbi of Algiers, where he died about 1410. In his decisions he is very orthodox, but distinguished by his humanitarian views. Thus he forced his congregations to rescind an order against the landing of further immigrants. His successor was Simeon ben Zemach Duran, whose responsa are collected under the title (Tashbez). He is supposed to have been the first rabbi who received a salary. In Italy, in the thirteenth century, Isaiah di Trani the Elder, and his grandson, Isaiah di Trani the Younger, flourished.

In the latter half of the fifteenth century Joseph Colon wrote a volume of responsa. His opponent was Elijah Kapsali. Of special interest in Colon's decisions is the case of the congregation of Nuremberg, in which he held that all German congregations were obliged to contribute toward the expenses of the trial of Israel Bruna, who was accused of complicity in the murder of a Christian child in 1477. In Germany the most important rabbi of the fifteenth century was Israel Isserlein of Marburg, 1400–1470, author of Terumat Ha-Deshen, a collection of responsa containing important historical notes. When the authorities in Breslau issued a law that Jews had to swear with uncovered head and by the name Yahve, he permitted it, provided it was not meant as an attempt to convert the Jews.

The German and French rabbis in the thirteenth century were characterized by their strict adherence to authority and rigorous view of the law. The most prominent is Judah ben Samuel Hechasid, author of "Sefer Hasidim." Eleazar ben Jehudah of Worms, a descendant of the Kalonymos family, and author of Rokeah (druggist), is a type of this ascetic school. Another is Moses of Coucy, author of a compendium of the 613 commandments Sefer Mizwot Haggadol, abbreviated Semag.

In the thirteenth century the study of Kabbala received strong impetus from Isaac, the blind, son of Rabed. His disciples were Ezra and Ezriel; their disciple was Ramban, and he introduced Kabbala into his commentary on the Pentateuch. About 1390 Moses of Leon wrote the Zohar, a Kabbalistic Midrash on the Pentateuch, which he claimed was written by Simeon ben Yohai, disciple of Akiba, and discovered by him in a cave. It is written in Aramaic.

CHAPTER VII

THE PERIOD OF IMPROVEMENT (1492-1791)

THE Jews of Spain went to Turkey, North Africa, Oriental countries, and especially to Palestine. They came in such numbers that their language, the so-called Ladino, became the language of the Jews in these countries, taking the place of Arabic and Greek. Sultan Bajazed II, 1481–1513, is reported to have said that he could not understand why Ferdinand of Spain should be called a wise king, since he had impoverished his own country and enriched Turkey. Jews stood very high at Court. Joseph Hamon was physician to Sultans Bajazed II and Selim I (1512–1520) and his son, Moses Hamon, to Sultan Soliman II (1520–1566). Joseph Mendes (died 1579) and his aunt, Gracia, whose daughter Reyna he had married, were Marranos who had fled from Spain to Antwerp, then to Venice, and finally to Constantinople. Joseph was a special favorite of the Sultan, who forced the Republic of Venice to surrender the property of Donna Gracia, which had been confiscated. The Sultan made Joseph Duke of Naxos, and he seriously contemplated the establishment of a Jewish state there. Owing to Don Joseph's influence, the Pope was forced to free a number of Marranos who had been imprisoned in the Papal States and charged with apostasy. A number of Jews, prompted by Messianic expectations, founded settlements in Jerusalem and Safed.

In Italy the condition of the Jews changed for the worse. Venice established the first ghetto, called thus after the gun foundry "Gietto" in the vicinity. At the end of the fifteenth and the beginning of the sixteenth century the Popes employed Jewish physicians, such as Bonet del Lattes under Leo X. But Paul IV and Pius V issued oppressive laws against the Jews, restricting their commercial activity to trading in cast-off clothing, enforcing the marks of distinction, Jew Badges, and ordering the censorship of Hebrew literature. The reaction against Protestantism and the foundation of the Jesuit order further tended to make the condition of the Jews still worse. The Council of Trent, 1563, prohibited the Talmud altogether, but later on modified its decree to the effect that the word Talmud should not be printed on the title page of the work and that every edition should be submitted to the ecclesiastic censor aided by Jewish converts. Prominent among the latter were Elijah and Solomon Romano, grandsons of Elijah Levita.

The Italian Jews, in order to obviate the dangers arising from informations against Jewish literature, decided in 1564 that no book should be printed without the consent of three prominent rabbis and the trustees of the congregation in the district where the press was located. By these measures the Hebrew printing trade, which had flourished in Italy during the first half of the sixteenth century, was ruined and the press transferred to Poland. There, owing to the low state of industry, the art of printing declined.

The frequent expulsions and the constant oppressions fostered Messianic hopes. In 1507 a Messianic pretender arose in Northern Italy. His name was

Asher Lemlein. Of the particulars of his career we
know nothing. Of greater importance is the appearance of a man who called himself David Reubeni in
Venice, 1522. He pretended to be the brother of the
reigning king of the tribe of Reuben, living in Arabia, and planned an alliance of the Christian powers
against the Mohammedans. For this he pledged the
aid of the ten tribes living there. The Pope sent him
to Portugal, where he made the acquaintance of Solomon Molcho, a young Marrano, who returned with
Reubeni to Italy, preached and prophesied there and
became a favorite of the Pope. The Jews feared the
results of his eccentricities and denounced him to the
authorities as an apostate from Christianity, but
the Pope shielded him. Finally both went to Germany
in 1530, where they hoped to win Charles V to their
plans. They were imprisoned; Molcho, as an apostate, was burned at the stake and Reubeni sent to
Portugal, where every trace of him was lost. Who he
was is not known. He seems to have travelled in the
East, and probably was an Arab.

The Reformation of 1517 at first influenced the condition of the Jews for the better. The accusations
that the Jews desecrated hosts ceased. As late as
1492 a number of Jews were burned for this supposed
crime at Sternberg in Mecklenburg. In 1510, thirty-
nine Jews were burned at Berlin for the same cause.
But aside from this Protestantism in itself stood for
religious toleration. Luther, in the beginning of his
career, spoke of the Jews as "cousins of our Lord,"
who should be treated with kindness. He thought
that his purified Christianity would win them over,
but, toward the end of his life, when he had failed in

his efforts and was embittered for other reasons, he wrote two pamphlets filled with invective against the Jews. In these he advocated the confiscation of their property, the destruction of their synagogues, and the forcible baptism of their children. Still more bitter than Luther's attacks were those of John Eck, his Catholic opponent.

It seems, however, that the Reformation increased the number of Jewish converts. Prominent among these was Emanuel Tremellius, an Italian, who first became a monk and then a Protestant. He was a friend of Calvin, and translated the Bible for him into Latin. He also translated Calvin's Catechism into Hebrew. Another convert was Luke Helic, who assisted the Moravian Brethren in translating the Bible into the Slavic language. A calumniator of Judaism was Antonius Margaritha, the son of a rabbi of Ratisbon, named Jacob Margaliot, who in 1530 wrote a libel on Judaism. Characteristic was the act of the Protestant Landgrave, Louis of Hesse, who advised the suppression of an anti-Jewish book, "Jüdenfeind," by Nigrinus (1570) saying that the same arguments might just as well be used by Catholics against Protestants.

The Renaissance, which produced the Reformation, also had a favorable effect on the position of the Jews. When John Pfefferkorn, a convert from Judaism, in 1506 accused the Jews of blaspheming Jesus in their prayers and in their literature, and proposed the confiscation of all their books, John Reuchlin, a famous diplomat and expert Hebrew scholar, rendered an opinion in their favor. The Dominicans of Cologne, among them a former rabbi, Victor von

Karben, whose tool Pfefferkorn had been, made the latter's cause their own, but did not succeed. In Frankfort-on-the-Main, where the books had been confiscated, they were ordered to be returned to their owners, and a long and bitter controversy, in which both parties engaged in vile attacks, ensued. In the meantime the Reformation intervened; and the Pope, who had been appealed to, ended the matter by an order in 1516 that both parties should keep their peace. He reversed this decision in favor of the Dominicans in 1520.

Such occasions as the calumniations of Pfefferkorn and others showed the arbitrariness of municipalities and lords in the treatment of the Jews, and pointed out the advisability of Jews appointing an advocate, "Shtadlan," who would always defend their rights when necessary. One of the most famous of these was Josel Rosheim (1478–1554) who was originally appointed as their advocate by the Jews of Alsace, and often acted in behalf of all the Jews of Germany, here and there arbitrating dissensions in congregations. He obtained various charters from Emperor Charles V, in which protection to the Jews was promised. Among these stipulations, one issued in 1530 is of special interest. The Emperor prohibited the expulsion of Jews from his territory without his consent. This rule, however, was not even observed in the immediate possessions of the German rulers. At various times Ferdinand I, brother of Charles V, and German Emperor (1522–1564) ordered expulsions from Austria in 1557, and in 1541 and 1561 from Bohemia; they were hardly ever carried out. When the expulsion from Bohemia was decreed, Mordecai Meisels, a wealthy Jew of Prague, 1528–1601, and the descendant of the Italian family Soncino, which in 1513 established a printing press in Prague, went to Rome and obtained a bull from the Pope for the protection of the Jews. The law of expulsion from Bohemia was repealed. Meisels was in other ways a great benefactor of his co-religionists.

In Berlin, where the Jews had been expelled in 1510, Leopold (Lippold) was a physician and favorite of the Margrave Joachim II of Brandenburg. After the death of his master he was accused of having poisoned him and executed in 1573. A new refuge was opened to the Jews in Holland, when this country gained its independence from Spain. A family of fugitive Marranos is said to have been driven to Emden, Hanover, by unfavorable winds, and thence they were advised to go to Amsterdam (1593). Moses ben Uri of Emden followed them and instructed them in Judaism. Some other converts followed, among them monks, statesmen and scholars. One of the most prominent rabbis of Amsterdam was Menasseh ben Israel, who in 1654, tried to obtain from Cromwell official permission for the Jews to resettle in England, whence they had been expelled in 1290. A bill introduced into Parliament for the readmission failed to pass, but prominent jurists rendered an opinion that the expulsion was not a legal act. The Jews already in London were not molested, opened a synagogue and acquired a cemetery in 1660. Charles II was favorable to the Jews, some of whom had assisted him financially before he had ascended the throne; in 1664 he confirmed their right of residence.

About the middle of the seventeenth century a colony of Marranos from Amsterdam settled in Brazil, which was then under Dutch rule. When the Portuguese reconquered it (1654) the Jews were expelled and settled in the Dutch West Indies and New York, then New Amsterdam. Governor Stuyvesant objected to their landing, but the directors of the West India Company, among whom there were several Jews, overruled his decision. Meantime the Jews had settled in Rhode Island, where Roger Williams had promulgated full religious freedom in 1657.

In Amsterdam the Portuguese community combined strict traditional piety with secular learning and great commercial activity. To the Portuguese Jews, Amsterdam owes its importance as the center of the diamond trade. Uriel Acosta, who held high office in Spain and emigrated to Holland in order to openly profess Judaism, became imbued with deistic ideas, was tried as a heretic and did penance. Then, excommunicated as a backslider, he became despondent and, having attempted to kill Rabbi Saul Morteira, committed suicide in 1640. Baruch or Benedict Spinoza (1633–1677) was also excommunicated, but disregarded all attempts to bring him back to Judaism. He is the originator of a famous system of philosophy, called Pantheism or Monism, laid down in his principal work, the "Ethics." He also occupies a prominent place in the history of Biblical Criticism through his work, "Tractatus Theologico Politicus."

In 1666, the year which the Christian Millenarians regarded as Messianic by reason of a passage in Revelation xiii, 18, Judaism was stirred by Sabbatai Zebi of Smyrna, who proclaimed himself the Messiah.

Expelled from that city he went to Egypt, where he
received the enthusiastic support of Raphael Joseph, a
wealthy tax-farmer.   In Palestine, whither he went,
he found many admirers, and the prophet, Nathan
of Gaza, proclaimed him the true Messiah.   Being
denounced for high treason, Sabbatai was brought to
Constantinople and imprisoned in the fort of Abydos,
but the means supplied by his followers enabled him
to hold court like a prince.   Everywhere in Europe
the majority of the Jews believed him to be the Messiah.   The representatives of the Jews in Poland sent
two prominent rabbis as a committee to him, but
Nehemiah Hakohen, the Polish Kabbalist, who had
come to ascertain the truth, denounced him as an im-
postor.   Sabbatai Zebi was brought before the Sultan
to answer a charge of high treason; and, in order to
save his life, he turned to Islam.   The Sultan gave
him an office, and for ten years, until his death, he
remained in contact with the Jews.   Many of his
followers turned to Islam, and still exist as a special
sect called Donmah in Salonica.   Others of his followers who remained true to Judaism formed a mystic community, which adopted the name of Hasidim.
They were excommunicated by the most prominent
rabbis, but progressed rapidly, although many of
them were unmasked as frauds.   Nehemiah Hayon, an
Oriental, wrote a book in which he taught the doctrine of the Trinity (1712) and Jacob Frank, a Polish
Jew, formed a Judæo-Christian sect.   The latter was
supported by those who wished to convert the Jews
to Christianity, and lived in princely style in Offen-
bach, where he died in 1793.

The center of Hasidism was in Podolia and Volhy-

nia; Israel Besht, 1695–1760, may be considered as its
founder.   His work was continued by his disciples,
among whom Baer Mezdzyrzecz (1700–1772) was the
most prominent.   Later Nahman of Bratzlav (1779–
1810) developed the theory of miraculous powers of
healing granted to favored individuals and the mystic
interpretation of the Bible and the Rabbinic com-
mands.   They still have a great number of devotees
in parts of Austrian and Russian Poland.

Persecutions in the seventeenth century are of rarer
occurrence than in former times.   The most serious
one was that which, with several interruptions, lasted
from 1648 to 1655, and the leader of which was the
Cossack captain Chmelnicki.   The Cossacks, who were
under the sovereignty of the Polish king, rebelled
against their masters, and the Jews had to suffer,
partly because they were unable to protect themselves,
and partly because, as tax-farmers, they had been the
instrument of the extortion practised by the Polish
nobles.   Thousands were massacred, and since that
time the 20th of Sivan is observed as a fast-day in
Poland.   They fled in all directions, and many great
Talmudists among them became rabbis in Western
Europe.

The Jesuits in Poland and in those places where the
Catholic Church had succeeded in crushing the Reformation became very powerful and fostered hatred
of the Jews, often resulting in mob violence.   In 1664
such a massacre occurred in Lemberg.   The Jews
were accused of the murder of Christians; similar
charges were often made.   In 1659 two prominent
Jews were put to death on Rosh Hashanah in Rossieny,
Lithuania, under the charge of ritual murder; in

1694 Lazarus Abeles and a friend of his were imprisoned in Prague, charged with having killed the son of Abeles, who wanted to become a Christian. Abeles hanged himself and his friend was cruelly put to death. In Vienna and Prague mission services, which the Jews were compelled to attend every Sabbath, were held by the Jesuits since 1630. In 1670 Emperor Leopold I expelled the Jews from Vienna, influenced partly by the hatred of the citizens and partly by the bigotry of the Empress, a Spanish princess. Some of the refugees were given permission by the Elector Frederick William of Brandenburg to settle in Berlin. At about the same time Halle, Halberstadt and Dessau were opened to them. In 1670 Herz Levi of Metz was accused of having murdered a Christian child and was put to death. His innocence was afterwards proved.

Peculiar to the history of the seventeenth and eighteenth centuries were the court Jews, Hof-Jude, Hof-factor, Minister-Resident. Prominent among them were Elijah Gomperz of Cleve, Moses Benjamin Wolf of Dessau, Jost Libman of Berlin, Behrendt Lehman of Dresden, and Samuel Oppenheimer and Samson Wertheimer of Vienna. These Jews did service as jewelers, bankers, general brokers and army contractors, and, as such, were exempt from Jewish taxes and certain disabilities. They possessed great influence, which they used to good advantage for their fellow-Jews. Samuel Oppenheimer, who died in 1703, obtained from Emperor Leopold an order of confiscation of an anti-Jewish book, "Entdecktes Judenthum," by J. A. Eisenmenger (1700), which, up to date, has served as a repertory for anti-Semitic writers.

In 1614 a serious riot broke out in Frankfort-on-

the-Main, led by the guilds, which accused the patri-
cians controlling the municipal council of partiality
to the Jews. The council, aided by imperial troops,
succeeded in suppressing the rebellion after considerable difficulty. Vincent Fettmilch, the leader, was
quartered, his home demolished, and his family
expelled from the city. Other ringleaders were
beheaded. While the city council thus showed its
sincere intention to have the law respected even with
regard to the Jews, the new legal regulation for the
Jews of Frankfort, "Juden-Staettigkeit," was a speci-
men of mediæval ideas, maintaining the usual restrictions on occupation, marriage, residence and quite a
number of measures, like the yellow badge, meant to
disgrace a Jew. It remained in force until 1807.

The political condition of the Jews at this time
nevertheless shows steady improvement, although their
threatened expulsion from the city of Metz and their
actual expulsion from Vienna and the province of
Lower Austria in 1670 were a relapse into the conditions of the fifteenth century. Still, such events are
local and few and far between; on the other hand, an
improvement is manifest in various instances where
Jews were admitted to countries or cities from which
they had been expelled in mediæval times. Particularly important was their settlement in Hamburg and
Berlin at this time. In Hamburg the municipal council gave to some Portuguese Marranos, who came
there to escape from the Inquisition, the right of residence in spite of clerical protest. The first settlers
were soon followed by Jews from Germany in the
course of the seventeenth century, and finally (1710),
they formed a legally-organized congregation. Simi-

larly Portuguese Jews had found a haven of refuge in various cities of Southern France, although there in a Catholic country they had to conceal their Judaism.

In Berlin and the Margravate of Brandenburg, the Elector Frederick William I allowed some Jews, expelled from Vienna, to settle in his states on their plea that they were persecuted for conscience' sake (1671). Still more important was the readmission of the Jews to England by Cromwell in 1654; and, although the bill for their readmission did not pass, their settlement was quietly overlooked and declared by jurists to be legally justified. Another new country was opened to Jewish settlement by the end of the sixteenth century when the Spanish Netherlands had made themselves independent of the Spanish crown. The constitution of the new country was based on perfect religious freedom, and naturally fugitives from the Inquisition were among the first to avail themselves of this opportunity. They were soon joined by the settlers from other countries, and in the seventeenth century Amsterdam was one of the leading Jewish communites of the world.

The greatest importance, however, attaches to the settlement of the Jews in the New World. While in the Spanish colonies there was not only no religious liberty but even persecutions of Marranos culminating in autos-da-fe, as in the mother country, the conquest of Brazil by the Dutch in 1624 resulted in the first organized Jewish community on the American continent. The loss of Brazil in 1654 forced the Jews to emigrate, and some settled in the Dutch and British possessions in Central and South America, Surinam, Curacoa and Jamaica. But the most important settle-

ment was that of New York in 1654. The intolerance
of the Dutch governor Stuyvesant drove some of the
newcomers to Newport, R. I. (1657), where Roger
Williams had proclaimed full religious liberty.

In 1733 some Portuguese Jews from England availed
themselves of the opportunity created by James Ogle-
thorpe, who made Georgia an asylum for convicts who
were willing to reform. They sent some of their poor
to Savannah. As the governor was unfavorable to
the settlement of the Jews, fearing that their presence
would prejudice the success of the colony, some Jews
went to South Carolina, for which the philosopher
John Locke had drafted a liberal constitution (1697).
He expressly declared equal rights for non-Christians.
They formed a congregation at Charleston in 1750,
for a long time the most flourishing Jewish settlement
in the territory now comprised in the United States.
Yet up to the end of the eighteenth century only six
Jewish communities are known: New York, Newport,
R. I., Savannah, Ga., Charleston, S. C., Philadelphia,
and Lancaster, Pa. These Jews took part in the
American Revolution, and their patriotism was expressly recognized in the reply of George Washington
to their addresses of congratulation when he was
elected President.

An English law of 1740 gave to the Jews in the
American colonies full rights of naturalization, also
extended to Canada when it became a British possession. The growth of Jewish population was slow and
did not begin until the reactionary governments of
Europe, after the July revolution of 1830, made the
hope of any improvement appear vain. Thus, since
1830 large streams of Jewish immigrants have settled

all over the United States.   Another far stronger current of immigration began in consequence of the persecutions in Russia in 1881.   The Jewish population
of America may now accordingly be figured at 2,000,-
000 souls.   In Spanish America the only settlement of
any consequence is in Argentine.

INTELLECTUAL AND LITERARY LIFE

The Reformation was promoted by the Renaissance,
essentially a critical examination of traditional views.
While this movement had not a very deep influence on
the Jews, it did not pass entirely unnoticed.   Elijah
Mizrahi, Chief Rabbi of Constantinople (1455–1525),
took notice of the Copernican system, and in his super-
commentary on Rashi, tried to harmonize this modern
conception of the cosmos with Rabbinic statements.
He also wrote a text-book of arithmetic, a commentary
on Euclid's elements, an astronomical book, besides
various Talmudic works.

More evident is the influence on Elijah Levita,
born in Neustadt-an-der-Aisch, Bavaria, 1468, died in
Venice, 1549.   Elijah Levita was a teacher of many
prominent Christian theologians, both Catholic and
Protestant, then very much interested in the study
of Hebrew.   He wrote various works on Hebrew
grammar, among them "Bahur" (1518), a glossary of
Rabbinic words, "Tishbi" (1541), and a book on the
Massorah, "Massoret ha-Massoret" (1548), in which
he laid down the bold and since that time generally-
accepted theory that the vowel points and accents
were not invented until the eighth century.   He was
also a writer of popular works, translated the Psalms
into Judæo-German and published the Bobo book, a

translation of an Italian romance based on the English
story of "Sir Bevis of Hampton," underlying Shake-
speare's "Hamlet" (1540).

Another exponent of the Renaissance was Azariah
dei Rossi of Ferrara (1511-1578), who in his work,
"Meor Enayim," a collection of critical essays, defended the theory that the Talmudic writings are not
authoritative on matters of history and science, but
merely on Rabbinic law.   Joseph Solomo del Medigo,
born in Crete, 1591, died at Prague, 1655, was an am-
biguous character and adventurer, a wanderer during most of his life.   In his work, "Elim" (1629), he
had the courage to criticize Rabbinic theology, and
especially the Kabbala.   Leon Modena of Venice
(1571–1648), who was a very prolific author, went
still further, attacking the Rabbinic law as in many
instances incongruous with the Bible, and recommend-
ing a change of the religious practices.   In the works
which he published he merely indicated his liberal
ideas; he clearly stated them in works that remained
unpublished for two centuries.

In Italy, where secular education was not held in
such abhorrence as was the case in Northern Europe,
in the seventeenth century two women wrote Italian
poetry and made translations from Hebrew.   These
are Deborah Ascarelli and Sarah Copia Sullam,.   An
attempt to rationalize Talmudic passages was made
as early as the beginning of the sixteenth century.
Jacob ibn Habib, who was among the exiles from Spain,
settled in Constantinople, and collected the Haggadic
passages of the Talmud, with the intention of publishing them with an apologetic commentary. He
died in 1516 after having finished only part of his

work; it was edited after his death by his son. It is even now, as "En Jacob," a very popular book for the study of Talmudic ethics.

While on one side there was a liberal tendency noticeable in Rabbinic Judaism, on the other a consolidation of the Rabbinic legalism and a progress of mysticism were noticeable. Joseph Caro (1488–1575), a native of Spain who toward the end of his life lived in Safed, Palestine, compiled a brief compendium of the Rabbinic law, "Shulhan Aruk." It was printed during the author's lifetime in Venice in 1564, and often reprinted afterwards. The author followed the arrangement of Jacob ben Asher, but otherwise is quite independent. It was his object to give the whole Rabbinic law in one volume, without showing its development and without regard to different opinions. He prepared himself for his work by writing exhaustive commentaries on the codes of Maimonides and Jacob ben Asher. During his lifetime the book was annotated by Moses Isserls of Cracow (1520–1572), who called his notes "Mappah" (tablecloth). It was his object to lay down the practice of the German Jews, neglected by Joseph Caro as a rule. This codification was strongly attacked by some of the more liberal rabbis of the time. Solomon Luria (1500–1573), rabbi of Lublin, but of German descent, took a more critical view of the old sources, although apart from legal decisions he proclaimed his absolute faith in traditions and condemned the liberal tendencies of Abraham ibn Esra and Maimonides.

A strong opponent of Azariah Dei Rossi was Loewe Ben Bezalel (1530–1609), rabbi of Posen and Prague and the hero of many legends. He maintained the ab-

solute belief in Rabbinic authority in every respect.
In spite of occasional opposition the "Shulhan Aruk"
soon attained general popularity and was considered
an authoritative book, to which many prominent
rabbis, as Abraham Gombiner, Sabbatai Cohen and
David Halevi added their glosses. These were in the
later editions added to the "Shulhan Aruk," the
authority of which is indicated by the fact that the
glossaries are called "Aharonim" (epigones).

The sufferings which Jews had to endure during the
fifteenth century and of which the expulsion from
Spain and Portugal was the culmination, were the
cause of a strengthening of mysticism. Particularly
in Palestine, to which quite a number of Spanish Jews
were drawn by Messianic hopes, such a center was
formed. In Safed, where Joseph Caro wrote his "Shulhan Aruk," a number of disciples gathered around
Isaac Luria, who preached a religion based on the belief in the mysterious. He did not write, but numerous disciples put his ideas in writing. Among them
were Hayyim Vital, who was considered a worker
of miracles, and Elijah de Vidas, whose work, "The
Beginning of Wisdom," became a favorite book for
edification. Another Kabbalistic author of the same
circle was Solomon Halevi Alkabez, best known by
his popular Sabbath hymn, "Lekah Dodi," which also
has a Kabbalistic tendency.

German Jews came to Palestine to join the circle
of mystics. One was Isaiah Horowitz (1550–1630),
who had been rabbi of Frankfort-on-the-Main and
Prague. Of his works a large Kabbalistic compendium, "The Two Tablets of the Covenant" (Shelah),
became very popular. Abstracts of it were made and

translated into Judæo-German. Even in Italy, where secular culture was far more general among Jews than in any other country in Europe, Kabbala had a strong hold on the people. A great enthusiast for the doctrine of mysticism was Moses Hayyim Luzzatto (1707–1747), who wrote allegorical dramas in Hebrew, one of which, "Praise to the Righteous," is a masterpiece of modern Hebrew literature. His ethical treatise, "The Path of the Righteous," is also deservedly popular. He went to Palestine hoping to receive prophetic inspiration there, and died at the age of forty of the plague.

Talmudic literature monopolized the activities of the German and Polish Jews, the latter being considered the leaders in this line and filling most of the Rabbinic positions in Western Europe during the seventeenth and eighteenth centuries. Among the most prominent dialecticians may be mentioned Jacob Joshua of Lemberg (1680–1756), rabbi of Frankfort-on-the-Main, Aryeh Loeb of Minsk, rabbi of Metz (1700–1786), Ezekiel Landau (1713–1793), rabbi of Prague, and Jonathan Eybeschuetz (1690–1764), rabbi of Metz and Altona, whose works show the highest development in this branch. Already in the eighteenth century a sounder development of Rabbinic studies, showing the beginnings of criticism and an interest in historical and archæological questions, began.

Among those who led to the scientific presentation of Rabbinic literature in modern times are to be mentioned Jair Hayyim Bacharach (1634–1702), rabbi of Worms, of whose works very little has been preserved but who was interested in the scientific presentation

of Rabbinic theology as the theory of oral tradition,
and Jacob Emden (1696–1776), the bitter opponent of
Jonathan Eybeschuetz, who gathered historical material on Sabbatai Zebi, and the mystics who followed
him and had the boldness, although a believer in Kabbala, to state that the Zohar, as we possess it, is not
the work of Simeon ben Johai. An emancipation
from the strict Rabbinic dialectics by better attention
to correct Rabbinic texts and to the study of philologi-
cal and archæological questions is found in the works
of Joseph Steinhart (1706–1776), rabbi of Fuerth,
Isaiah Pick (1720–1799), and Elijah of Wilna (1720–
1797).

The sufferings of the Jews in Spain stimulated interest in historical literature and various authors,
chiefly prompted by a desire to keep up the courage of
the Jews in the midst of persecutions, wrote historical
works. Among them may be mentioned Gedaliah ibn
Yahya, an Italian who wrote the "Chain of Tradition," Solomon ibn Verga, a Spaniard who emigrated
to Turkey and wrote "Shebet Jehudah," Joseph Cohen
of Avignon, who·wrote "The Valley of Weeping,"
and Samuel Usque, who wrote a work in Portuguese
called "Consolations in Tribulation," all of the sixteenth century. Somewhat later David Gans (died at
Prague in 1617) wrote a dry compilation of events in
Jewish and general history under the title "Zemah
David."

To the seventeenth century belongs the Oriental,
David Conforte, his "Kore Hadorot" being chiefly
valued for its accounts of Rabbinic literature in the
Orient. Jehiel Heilprin of Minsk, eighteenth century,
wrote a history in the style of a chronicle, beginning

with Creation. It shows a naive belief in the historic-
ity of the Midrash but is very valuable by reason of
its collection of historic passages from Rabbinic literature.   Secular education was slowly beginning to find
its way among the Jews.   Quite a number of German
Jews studied medicine in Italy, chiefly from a practical point of view.   Tobias Cohen of Metz (1652–1729)
studied in Frankfort-on-the-Oder, being supported by
the Elector of Brandenburg.   In his later years he
lived in the Orient, where he wrote a compilation on
various scientific subjects, ''Maaseh Tobiyah.'' In this
he shows sound knowledge of medicine.

CHAPTER VIII

THE PERIOD OF EMANCIPATION FROM 1791.

IN the middle of the eighteenth century a slow but marked improvement in the condition of the Jews is noticeable. To some extent this is due to the change in the economic life of the Jews, many of whom were engaged in manufacturing pursuits and in such mercantile enterprises as were of noticeable benefit to the state. Some Jews were farmers of the tobacco monopoly, in many states an important part of the revenue, others engaged in various manufacturing enterprises and thus received privileges which exempted them from the disabilities imposed on other Jews. This was the case in Prussia, where Jewish enterprises created the flourishing textile industry in and near Berlin. One of these manufacturers was Bernhard Isaac, in whose house Moses Mendelssohn lived first as tutor and then as bookkeeper. Frederick the Great gave to some Jews the same rights as Christian merchants, although he was in general not well disposed toward the Jews, and would not allow them to engage in agriculture or ship-building. Aaron Elias Seligmann established a large tobacco manufactory in Laimen, Bavaria, in 1779, which gave occupation to many hands; for his merit in developing industry the King of Bavaria bestowed a baronetcy on him in 1814. Israel Hönig was farmer of the tobacco monopoly

in Austria, and was in 1789 knighted by Emperor
Joseph II.

The distinctions bestowed on individual Jews, however, did not improve the condition of the masses.
The progress of liberal ideas made this question a
matter of serious concern for legislators.   In England
a bill giving the Jews political rights was passed in
1753, but aroused such opposition among the populace
that the government found itself compelled to repeal
it in the same year.   Of more permanent value were
the measures of the humane Joseph II of Austria
(1780–1790).   In various legislative acts, and especially in the so-called "Toleranz-Edict" of January 2,
1782, he laid down the principle that the Jews should
be treated like human beings.   Although they were
still under considerable restrictions, their lot was in
many ways improved, and the Emperor laid special
stress on their education.   As a tangible evidence of
the improvement in their condition the abrogation of
the poll tax, "Leibzoll," the Jew badge and Jew taxes
may be noted.   The abolition of these mediæval discriminations, which were based on the principle that
the Jew was a foreign and injurious element of the
population, became more and more general by the end
of the eighteenth century.

France abolished the poll tax in 1784.   As early as
1781 the Academy of Metz offered a prize for the best
essay on the improvement of the Jews.   The prize was
won by Abbé Grégoire, a Catholic priest, who advocated the abrogation of all Jewish disabilities.   About
the same time Christian F. Dohm, an official in the
Prussian war department, wrote an essay on the civil
improvement of the Jews, in which he likewise advo-

cated the granting of full equality to the Jews. This principle became for the first time a fact when on September 27, 1791, the French National Assembly passed a bill giving the Jews full civic and political equality with other citizens.

When the French rule spread over adjacent countries this was everywhere adopted. Such was the case in Holland in 1796, and in all parts of Germany which directly or indirectly came under French influence. In Cologne, where for nearly four hundred years no Jew had been permitted to reside, Jews began to settle in 1798. In Mayence the population tore down the gates of the ghetto in 1798, and this was done in Rome when the French ruled there. In Frankfort-on-the-Main, where the Jews labored under cruel discriminations, their condition was considerably improved in 1807 by an edict of the Grand Duke, Baron von Dahlberg, and in 1811 they were given full civil equality. Even reactionary countries like Prussia could not resist the current of the time, and the edict of March 11, 1812, declared the Jews to be citizens, gave them freedom of residence and occupation and the right to professorships in the universities; and although it withheld from them political rights, it promised to grant them such in the future.

Jews have been drafted into the army in Austria since 1787, and in Prussia since 1812; but numerous Jews joined the army as volunteers and distinguished themselves by acts of bravery during the wars of liberation. In 1809 the Austrian Jew, Israel Hönig, was made lieutenant for bravery on the battlefield of Aspern, and a few years afterwards was promoted to the rank of captain. In Prussia several Jews were promoted to the rank of officers during the Napoleonic wars.

Meantime reaction began to set in.   Napoleon, who as commander of the army in the Orient in 1798, had called upon the Jews to join his army and conquer Palestine, changed his policy.   Moved by complaints against the business methods of the Jews, he called an assembly of Jewish notables in 1806 and laid before them twelve questions, including whether the Jews considered themselves Frenchmen, whether their law permitted them to take usurious interest from non-Jews and whether intermarriage with Christians would be permitted.   The answers given by this body of men were satisfactory, and the Emperor in 1807 established a Sanhedrin to ratify these principles and form a supreme ecclesiastic authority for all the Jews of the world.   While thus apparently showing favor to the Jews, he issued a law in 1808 which imposed some restrictions on the freedom of trade of the Jews of Alsace.   With his downfall, however, a general reaction set in.   Some states repealed the laws which had given full freedom to the Jews, while others, among them Prussia, limited the efficacy of these laws by interpretation.

In Rome, where the rule of the Pope was reinstated, all oppressive measures were put in force again.   In Hamburg and Luebeck, where, during the French rule, the Jews had enjoyed full equality, the former restrictions were partly reintroduced.   From Luebeck the Jews were unconditionally expelled in 1816.   In some cities of Bavaria attacks on the Jews were organized by the mob under the cry of "Hep-hep" in 1819, and an article of the Congress of Vienna of

1815, which declared that the Jews should retain all the rights they had acquired during the time of transition, became practically a dead letter.

The July Revolution of 1830 strengthened liberal ideas and brought the Jewish question up for discussion in various Parliaments, particularly in Southern Germany. In Baden and Bavaria the petition for the improvement of the condition of the Jews was regularly met with the demand that the Jews should first show their willingness to assimilate with their environment by a change of their religious beliefs and practices. Legislation made very little progress, and in some instances new reactionary measures were introduced. King Frederick William III of Prussia in 1836 ordered that Jews should not have any Christian names. The decisive change came about after the French Revolution in 1848.

By and by all states of Western Europe recognized in their constitutions the full civil and political equality of the Jews, and in the [Parliaments which were elected on this basis, Jews were members. Gabriel Riesser (1806–1864) was one of the vice-presidents of the National Assembly in Frankfort. The first Austrian Parliament had five Jewish members and the Diet of Bavaria two. When the storm passed away, a reactionary spirit again took hold, although the liberties granted to the Jews were not entirely repealed. Some countries like Austria suspended the constitution, while others like Prussia interpreted it in a sense which rendered nugatory some of the rights given to the Jews in theory. This, however, was mostly the case with regard to the right of holding official positions. Civic equality and the right to vote at elections and hold elective offices remained uncontested.

Finally toward the end of the 'sixties even these disabilities were removed. The Austrian constitution of 1867 granted to the Jews unrestricted equality. The law of the North German Federation of July 3, 1869, declared that every state must remove all disabilities imposed upon citizens on the ground of their religious belief. This law was embodied in the constitution of the German Empire in 1871. Sweden, which had admitted the Jews only at the end of the eighteenth century, and in 1838 still restricted their residence to four cities, granted them full equality in 1870. Switzerland, while a republic, had for a long time restricted the Jews to two places in the Canton of Aargau. Not until 1878 were they given full equality with other citizens. Norway had, until 1851, a law on its statute-book which prohibited even the temporary residence of Jews in the country.

England made slow but steady progress. In 1830 the first attempt was made to give the Jews political rights, a year previously the disabilities imposed on Christian dissenters having been removed. In 1833 Francis H. Goldsmid was admitted to the bar, and in 1835 David Salomons was elected sheriff of London and Middlesex, the first municipal office held by a Jew. In 1845 he was elected alderman and in 1855 Lord Mayor of the city of London. The entrance of Jews to Parliament was opposed with great vehemence by the Conservative Party. In 1847 Baron Lionel de Rothschild was elected to Parliament, but could not take his seat because the prescribed oath contained "upon the true faith of a Christian." Not until 1858 was a bill passed which allowed a Jew to omit these words from the oath. His son, Baron Nathan de Rothschild, was in 1885 admitted as the first Jew to the House of Lords.

Only in the East of Europe restrictions continued. Czar Alexander I in 1804 issued a law which encouraged the Jews to take up agricultural pursuits and acquire secular knowledge. This step was isolated, and in the reign of Nicholas I (1825–1855) the Jews were subjected to terrible persecutions, the worst of which was that children were forcibly taken from the houses of their parents and brought up in barracks as soldiers to serve twenty-five years after they had reached the age required for the army. Under Alexander II (1855–1881) a slow improvement in exceptional cases took place. Jews who engaged in manufacturing or business enterprises, skilled mechanics and those who had received a college education, were exempt from most of the disabilities imposed on the masses, but the condition of the latter was not changed. They were still restricted in their rights of residence and occupation and excluded from all political rights.

With the assassination of Alexander II a new era of persecutions began. This culminated in bloody riots, which spread over a great part of Southern Russia and were periodically repeated afterwards. The bloodiest persecutions were those of Kishineff and Homel in 1903, and of Odessa and a great many other cities in Southern Russia in 1905, and of Bialystok in 1906, when more than a thousand people lost their lives. Even further restrictions were introduced. Thus a law of May 3, 1882, prohibited the residence of Jews in rural districts and the acquisition of rural estates, and while in former times the acquisition of secular knowledge by Jews was encouraged by the government, laws of December 5, 1886, and July 6, 1887, restricted the attendance of Jewish students at high schools and universities to a percentage ranging from three to ten. While the Jews obtained the right to participate in the elections of the Duma, the Imperial Parliament, they have no right to participate in municipal elections and are represented in the municipal boards only by a few members who are appointed by the government. They are also excluded from the county boards, Zemstvo.

Similar conditions prevail in Rumania. When that country gained its autonomy in 1856, it not only denied to the Jews political rights but declared them to be foreigners. Frequent mob attacks and arbitrary treatment on the part of the courts and the officials made them practically outlaws. A hope for improvement seemed to loom up when in 1878 the Congress of Berlin embodied an article in the treaty which compelled the newly founded sovereign and autonomous states of Servia, Bulgaria and Rumania to remove from their statute-books all laws discriminating against citizens on the ground of religious belief. They complied with this requirement, but Rumania availed itself of a ruse by which the law was practically rendered nugatory. By declaring the Jews to be foreigners, and naturalizing some Jews, it apparently complied with the law, while almost all the 250,000 Jews of the country remained in their former state of misery, enhanced by new regulations restricting their economic freedom.

It looked in 1878 as if Europe had guaranteed the fair treatment of the Jews even in countries of oppression; opposition began in popular ranks, and in the same year anti-Semitism arose as a new name for hostility toward the Jews. This first made itself felt in Germany through the foundation of the Christian Socialist party in 1878, started with the avowed object of withdrawing from the Jews their political rights, including that of holding public office and advocating the prohibition of the immigration of Jews.

From Germany the movement spread to Austria, where it first was taken up by the radical German party in 1883, and later on by the clericals. It spread then to Hungary and France, where the publication of Drumont's "La France Juive" in 1886 marks the beginning of the movement culminating in the Dreyfus case. Captain Alfred Dreyfus in 1894 was charged with high treason in order to stir up anti-Jewish feeling, and this was not abated until his innocence had finally been established in 1906. Another sign of an unfavorable change in the attitude of the masses toward the Jews was the revival of the blood accusation. When in 1840 it made its appearance in Damascus, where Jews were imprisoned and tortured for this cause, it seemed that such a return to mediæval barbarism was confined to the Orient. In 1882, however, it took place in Tisza-Ezlar, Hungary, and other cases followed in Western Europe: at Xanten, Germany, in 1891, at Konitz in 1899, and at Polna, Bohemia, in 1900.

The disappointment caused by the unlooked-for reaction manifested itself also in the attitude of the Jews with regard to their future. Soon after it had become evident that the condition of the Jews in Rumania would not be improved by the Treaty of Berlin, and after the bloody persecutions in Russia had destroyed the hope that Russia would slowly improve the condition of its Jews, a movement for the settlement of the Jews in Palestine began. In 1882 the foundation of a society, "Lovers of Zion," marked the beginning of a movement looking toward the resettlement of the Jews in Palestine. It assumed more systematic shape by the publication of "Der Judenstaat," by Theodor Herzl in 1896, which was followed in 1897 by the first Congress of Zionists convened at Basle, which declared in its platform the object to establish "a legally secured home for the Jewish people in Palestine." At the same time an unprecedented emigration took place from Russia and Rumania to free countries, particularly to the United States, Canada, Australia and South Africa, with a smaller but also considerable stream of emigration to England.

Baron de Hirsch attempted to regulate the emigration by turning it to Argentine, where he acquired large tracts of land in 1890. Indeed, agricultural settlements were founded there, although they did not realize the expectations of those who would have turned large masses of immigrants into that country.

In spite of the retrogressive movement which the history of the Jews seemed to present, Western Europe not only retained the principles enacted by the constitutions promulgated in and after 1848, but individual Jews have risen to prominence in political life. Almost all states of Western Europe have had Jews as members of their Parliaments, and some have ob-

tained prominent positions in the government service.
France had several Jews as ministers. Cremieux was
minister of justice in 1848, Godchaux and Achille
Fould served under Napoleon III, and Raynal under the
republic.   In Italy, Wollemborg was once and Luzzatti
six times minister of finance, and Joseph Ottolenghi
was minister of war.   In 1910 Luzatti became pre-
mier. Holland had repeatedly Jewish ministers, and
England saw in 1909 the first Jew, Herbert Samuel,
member of the cabinet.   The United States had a Jew
in the cabinet in the person of Oscar S. Straus, secretary of commerce and labor (1906–1909).   In the
Grand Duchy of Baden, Moritz Ellstaetter was minister of finance (1868–1893).   Quite a number of Jews
have occupied positions as judges, as professors at
universities, and in other public activities.

CULTURE

The improvement of the political conditions influenced the intellectual and social life of the Jews to a
considerable degree.   This is noticeable in their literature, education, religious life and finally in their communal organizations.

Moses Mendelssohn (1729–1786), of Dessau, came
as a boy to Berlin.   After a youth filled with hardship
he found employment in the house of a manufacturer,
first as tutor and then as bookkeeper.   His main
object was to raise Jews from their intellectual isolation.   He translated the Pentateuch, the Psalms and
some smaller books of the Bible into correct German,
and edited this work with a Hebrew commentary.   It
soon became popular and was the medium for teaching the young people the German language.   He also

defended Judaism against various attacks and presented its teaching in a German work, "Jerusalem." In his work on the Bible, he was assisted by various co-workers, among whom the most prominent is Naphtali Herz Wesel, who called himself Hartwig Wessely (1725–1805). The latter's epic on the life of Moses, patterned on Klopstock's "Messias," was written in elegant Hebrew verse, and became an inspiration to many other writers disgusted with the obscure and artificial style of Rabbinic Hebrew, and having a taste for literary beauty. An organ for such endeavors was presented by the publication of the first Hebrew magazine, "Meassef" (1784).

The progress of secular education made Hebrew literature soon disappear in Western Europe, but the influence of Wessely and his disciples made itself very strongly felt in the East of Europe, and particularly in the countries comprising the former kingdom of Poland. Their modern Hebrew writings introduced the young men to the knowledge of history and science, and gave them a taste for secular education and for a western conception of life. Isaac Bär Loewinson (1788–1860) wrote works in defense of Judaism, and advocated secular culture, patriotism, manual trades and the emancipation from mediæval conditions still existing in these countries. Marcus Aaron Guenzburg (1795–1846) worked chiefly as translator of popular works, such as juveniles like Campe's "Robinson Crusoe."

A more independent character was given to Hebrew literature by Abraham Mapu (1808–1867) who wrote two novels from Biblical life, "The Love of Zion," and "The Guilt of Samaria," and another describing the

102 HISTORY OF THE JEWS

life of the Jew in his Lithuanian home, "The Hypo-
crite." Mapu used Biblical Hebrew with great facil-
ity and became the father of a new development in
Hebrew and later in Yiddish, giving to Jewish literature a high literary character. He was followed by
Judah Loew (Leon) Gordon (1833–1892), whose satir-
ical poems not merely possess a value for the ease with
which the author handled the Hebrew language, but
have been a great force impressing upon the minds of
the Jews in Eastern Europe the defects of their intellectual isolation and the shortcomings of Rabbinic
teachings. Among the later poets Chayim Nachman
Bialik, born 1873, is the most popular. His elegy on
the massacre of Kishineff is one of the gems of
modern Hebrew literature.

Yiddish literature from its earliest beginnings in the
sixteenth century was mostly used as a vehicle for
the religious instruction of women and people of little
education or merely adapted and translated some of
the popular literature of the countries where its ex-
ponents lived. From the middle of the nineteenth
century it commenced to assume a more independent
character and thus secured a place in the world's history as is shown by the fact that some of its works were
translated into other European languages. Among
the novelists may be mentioned Shalom Jacob Abram-
owitsch (born 1836) who writes under the pseudonym,
"Mendele the bookseller," Shalom Rabinowitsch
(born 1859) and, the most popular of all, Isaac Loeb
Peretz (born 1851). A poet who presents the tragic
as well as the humorous side of the New York ghetto,
Morris Rosenfeld, born 1864, is to be mentioned; his
works have been translated into various European

languages. Of dramatists whose works have occasionally found their way to the German and English
stage there are Shalom Asch, and Jacob Gordin
(1853–1909), who deals with the life of Russian Jews
in America.

The disappearance of the social and intellectual
isolation in the life of the Jews created a special
literature which is called the ghetto novel. This
deals with the life of the Jews in the era of transition
from their isolation to modern culture. This literature began in Germany and its best known representatives are Aaron Bernstein (1812–1884), Leopold
Kompert (1822–1886), Karl Emil Franzos (1848–1904),
and, among Christians who view the life of the Eastern Jews with sympathy, Leopold von Sacher-Ma-
soch (1835–1895) and Eliza de Orzeska (1842–1910).
Sketches from the life of the Alsatian Jews were presented in French by Alexander Weill (1811–1898) and
in Danish by Meier Aaron Goldschmidt (1819–1887).
In the English language, Israel Zangwill, born 1864,
wrote novels dealing with the life of the foreign Jews
in England. Among his works "The Children of the
Ghetto" has obtained a place in the world's best literature. The English stories of Martha Wolfenstein
(1869–1906) deal with the life of European Jews.

A place in modern Jewish literature belongs to the
Jewish press as it has developed in the nineteenth century. The first Jewish periodical that had more than
an ephemeral existence was "Meassef," published in
Hebrew with some parts in German. It began to appear in 1784, and with some interruptions was kept
up until 1810. The oldest periodical still in existence
is the "Allgemeine Zeitung des Judentums," begun

by Ludwig Philippson, rabbi in Magdeburg, in 1837. It was followed by the "Archives Israélites" in 1840 in Paris, and by the "Jewish Chronicle" in 1841 in London. Of the numerous periodicals published in the United States, the oldest still existing is the "American Israelite," founded by Isaac M. Wise in Cincinnati in 1854.

The first Hebrew weekly, which dealt not only with Jewish affairs, was the "Hamaggid," founded by Lazarus Silbermann in Lyck, East Prussia, in 1858. The first Hebrew daily paper was the "Hazefirah," published first as a weekly in 1862 and afterwards as a daily from 1886. Quite a number of valuable magazines dealing with Jewish history and literature have been published since the middle of the nineteenth century in Hebrew and in various modern languages. "Wissenschaftliche Zeitschrift fuer Juedische Theologie" (1835–1840) and "Juedische Zeitschrift fuer Wissenschaft und Leben" (1862–1875) were both edited by Abraham Geiger; the "Monatsschrift fuer Geschichte und Wissenschaft des Judentums," begun by Zechariah Frankel in 1854, was discontinued in 1887 and has been republished since 1891. "Revue des Etudes Juives" dates from 1881; "Jewish Quarterly Review" appeared from 1888 to 1908. Of the Hebrew magazines there are "Kerem Hemed," of which nine volumes were published from 1833 to 1856, Bikure Ha-ittim (1820–1831), and "Haschiloach" since 1896.

Rabbinic literature of the older type, dealing with the law and Talmudic dialecticism has, also a great number of representatives during this period. Among the foremost may be named Moses Schreiber (Sofer),

born at Frankfort-on-the-Main in 1762, died as rabbi
of Presburg in 1839, and Akiba Eger (1761–1837).
In Western Europe this literature shows a steady
decline.   Of the authors whose life belongs entirely
to the nineteenth century may be mentioned Jacob
Ettlinger, rabbi of Altona (1798–1871), and Seligman
Bär Bamgerger, rabbi of Wuerzburg (1807–1878). Very
numerous, however, are the Rabbinic authors of Eastern Europe and the Orient, among whom Isaac Elha-
nan Spector, rabbi of Kovno (1810–1896), Hayim David
Hazan, rabbi of Jerusalem (1790–1868), Hayim Pa-
laggi, rabbi of Smyrna (1784–1868), and Hayim Hezekiah Medini (1834–1904), may be mentioned.

Already before Mendelssohn's time individual Jews
in Germany and Austria distinguished themselves in
literature and science.   But the education of the
masses was almost entirely confined to Bible and Talmud.   With the popularization of secular knowledge
the necessity for schools arose and the first institution
of this kind was founded in Berlin as the "Jewish
Free School" in 1778.   The efforts of Emperor Joseph
II to promote secular culture among the Jews of Austria led to the establishment of a primary school in·
Prague in 1782.   Others followed in different cities:
the Wilhelm Schule of Breslau was founded in 1791;
the Herzog Franz-Schule in Dessau in 1799.   Higher
schools were the Jacobson Schule in Seesen in 1801,
the Samson Schule in Wolfenbuettel in 1803, and the
Philanthropin in Frankfort-on-the-Main in the next
year.   Even in Eastern Europe, where religious fanaticism was bitterly opposed to secular education, such
schools came into existence like the one founded in
Tarnopol by Joseph Perls in 1815.   The Alliance

Israelite Universelle, founded in 1860, made it one of
its principal objects to establish schools for secular
education in the Orient, and it now has a great number of schools which it maintains in Turkey, Northern
Africa and Asia, extending from Palestine and Asia
Minor to Persia and Mesopotamia.

With the growing number of schools the need for
special training schools for Jewish teachers arose.
The first of these was founded in Berlin in 1825.
More important was the need for training schools for
rabbis.   The old method of education by which every
young man who devoted himself to study was a Talmudic scholar was discontinued in Western Europe.
On the other hand, it became necessary to give the
rabbis a more systematic training.   The first modern
school of this kind was established in Padua, then
under Austrian rule, in 1829.   Later the Yeshibah of
Metz was transformed into a Rabbinic seminary and
subsequently transferred to Paris.   In 1854 the Rabbinic seminary of Breslau was founded and this was
followed by the establishment of similar institutions
in European countries.   In 1875 the first Rabbinic
seminary in America, the Hebrew Union College of
Cincinnati, was opened.   In New York the Jewish
Theological Seminary was established in 1886.
Various educational institutions devoted to special
needs, such as the school for the deaf-mutes opened in
Nikolsburg in 1845, and later transferred to Vienna,
and the first Jewish institute for the blind established
in the latter city in 1872, deserve to be mentioned in
this connection.

The removal of the disabilities which kept the Jews
from agriculture and mechanical trades, and the de-

sire of the Jews to direct the young generation into such pursuits gave rise to quite a number of institutions all over the world devoted to these purposes. Several of these are located in the Orient and were founded or subventioned by the Alliance Israélite. It established the first agricultural school near Jaffa in Palestine in 1871. The Hebrew Technical Institute of New York, founded in 1884, the agricultural schools at Ahlem, founded 1893, at Woodbine, N. J., 1891, and at Doylestown, Pa., 1896, may be mentioned.

With the emancipation from Rabbinic studies a new development in Jewish learning took place. This showed itself in what is called the "Science of Judaism," and may be defined as a systematic study of Jewish history and literature. The pioneer in this work was Leopold Zunz (1794–1886) who wrote books on the history of Jewihs homiletics, on the synagogal poetry and various minor essays on all phases of Jewish literature. He found numerous followers, not merely in western Europe, but also in the East, and thus contributed largely to the intellectual elevation of the Jews.

In Eastern countries the first who wrote on these topics in Hebrew were Nahman Krochmal (1785–1840) and Solomon Loew Rapoport (1790–1867). The latter, inspired by the works of Zunz, was the author of biographies of prominent mediæval rabbis. In Italy we have Isaac Samuel Reggio (1784–1855) and Samuel David Luzzatto (1800–1865), who used the excellent collections of old Hebrew prints and manuscripts for the elucidation of the history of Jewish literature. The external side of the literature was presented in erudite form by the great bibliographer

Moritz Steinschneider (1816–1907). History in more readable form was written first by Isaac Marcus Jost (1795–1860), and then by Heinrich Graetz (1817–1891), the latter's work having gone through various editions and been translated into French, English, Hebrew and Yiddish. Numerous authors worked at the elucidation of portions of Jewish history and carefully edited old manuscripts. Thus they shed light on obscure parts of the Jewish past and showed the many-sided activity of the Jews during the long period of their history and their influence on all human activities.

In this connection the participation of the Jews in spiritual activity ought to be mentioned. We find them as authors, artists, inventors and scholars in all lines. Only the most prominent can be named. Ludwig Boerne, formerly Loeb Baruch (1784–1837), is one of the classic essayists of German literature. Heinrich Heine (1797–1856) is one of the greatest of lyric poets. Both Heine and Boerne became converted to Christianity. A classic author of village idyls is Berthold Auerbach (1812–1882). Among the greatest tragedians of the world are Eliza Rachel Felix (1821–1858), in her days the foremost actress on the French stage, and Adolf von Sonnenthal (1832–1909) considered the most prominent German actor of his time. Giacomo Meyerbeer (1791–1864) is one of the world's best known composers. Moritz Oppenheimer (1800–1881) was a prominent painter, and his scenes from Jewish life possess, besides their value as works of art, great worth as historic scenes. Marcus Antokolsky (1842–1902) is one of the most famous sculptors, and Joseph Israels (born 1824) and Max Liebermann (born 1849) are among the greatest painters of our age. In the lines of science and scholarly work the names of prominent Jews are too numerous to mention.

The great change in the life of the Jews and their education brought about the necessity of harmonizing their religious practices with their new life. Thus the reform movement began. The forces which promoted it were æsthetic, political and dogmatic. In the first class may be reckoned the efforts of Israel Jacobson (1769–1828). Although not a professional scholar he was a man of considerable Jewish learning, and his object was to make the services of the synagogue more attractive to the younger generation. The synagogue established by him in connection with the school which he founded in Seesen in 1810 was the first that introduced some of the reforms which since have been generally accepted, namely, a sermon in the vernacular and decorum and modern music.

In 1818 the first reform congregation was established in Hamburg. It was followed in 1824 by a similar organization in Charleston, S. C.; this, however, was soon dissolved. These synagogues introduced a ritual different from the one which had up to this time been generally in use. The most important changes were those which eliminated the belief in the return of the Jews to Palestine and consequently also in the restoration of the sacrificial cult. These were followed by an attempt to present systematically the teachings of modern Judaism and to apply the principles of the modern critical school to the whole of Jewish life, particularly the observance of the dietary and marriage laws.

The desire to work in harmony led to the convocation of Rabbinic assemblies, the first of which was held in Frankfort-on-the-Main in 1844. As the exponent of the most radical views Samuel Holdheim (1806–1860) is to be mentioned. It was his idea that Judaism had lost all its former national significance. On this basis the reform congregation of Berlin, whose first rabbi Holdheim was, was established in 1845, introducing for the first time solemn services on Sunday.

The most prominent scientific exponent of the reform idea was Abraham Geiger (1810–1874), one of the most prominent workers in scientific Jewish literature. He stood for a more historic conception of the reform principle, although as a Bible critic his position was advanced. His views were shared by two of the leading rabbis of America, David Einhorn (1809–1879) and Samuel Hirsch (1815–1889). They, together with Samuel Adler (1809–1891), represented the progressive ideas of German theology in America.

In 1842 reform was definitely introduced in the synagogue of Charleston, S. C., following the example set by the foundation of the West London Synagogue of British Jews the year previously. In America, however, reform took strongest hold and soon was accepted by the leading congregations composed of the native and the naturalized element. The most prominent figure in the popularization of this movement in America was Isaac Mayer Wise (1819–1900).

A more conservative view, usually spoken of as that of historic Judaism, was represented by Zechariah Frankel (1801–1875). He stood for freedom of thought in theoretical matters but advocated conservatism in worship and practice. Another division was formed by those who stood uncompromisingly for the preservation of the traditional Jewish life based on a strict belief in the divine origin of the Bible and the authenticity of Rabbinic interpretation, differing from the old school only in so far as they admitted secular education. The chief exponent of this thought was Samson Raphael Hirsch (1808–1888). In America his views were represented by Isaac Leeser (1806–1868) and Sabato Morais (1823–1897), while a compromising attitude was taken by Benjamin Szold (1829–1902) and Marcus Justrow (1829–1903). The traditional view of Judaism in the sense in which it had generally existed until the latter half of the eighteenth century, was restricted to the Orient and Eastern Europe and to congregations formed by recent immigrants from these countries in Western Europe and America. As a literary champion of this uncompromising attitude Hillel Lichtenstein (1815–1891) deserves mention.

One of the features of modern Jewish development is the communal organization rendered possible by the freedom of movement in religious, charitable and political activities. The Alliance Israélite Universelle deserves for this the first place. It was founded for the purpose of defending the interests of the Jews in countries of oppression and promoting their economic and moral as well as their intellectual status. This organization was followed by others with similar objects, the Israelitische Allianz of Vienna, started in 1873, the Anglo-Jewish Association, founded in 1871, and the Hilfsverein der deutschen Juden, in 1901.

Of the many organizations confined to particular

countries the Deutsch-Israelitischer Gemeinde-Bund, founded in 1869, and the Union of American Hebrew Congregations, established in 1873, deserve special mention.   Very numerous are the societies created for the promotion of the welfare of the Jews, and aside from the local institutions, like hospitals, homes for the aged, orphan asylums and sanitariums, the societies for the promotion of mechanical trades and agriculture are distinctly a product of the Jewish conditions of the nineteenth century.

Of organizations having a wider scope, the Jewish Colonization Association founded by Baron Moritz de Hirsch in 1891, has the greatest capital.   These schemes of colonization, to which the work done by the Zionist organizations and that contemplated by the Jewish Territorial Organization founded in 1905, have to be added, are as yet only in their infancy. In general, however, since the French Revolution there has been a steady progress of Jewish life in all directions.

INDEX